Library of
Davidson College

TEXTUAL HAUNTINGS

Studies in Flaubert's *Madame Bovary* and
Mauriac's *Thérèse Desqueyroux*

Edward J. Gallagher

University Press of America,® Inc.
Lanham · Boulder · New York · Toronto · Oxford

Copyright © 2005 by
University Press of America,® Inc.
4501 Forbes Boulevard
Suite 200
Lanham, Maryland 20706
UPA Acquisitions Department (301) 459-3366

PO Box 317
Oxford
OX2 9RU, UK

All rights reserved
Printed in the United States of America
British Library Cataloging in Publication Information Available

Library of Congress Control Number: 2005922593
ISBN 0-7618-3201-7 (clothbound : alk. ppr.)
ISBN 0-7618-3202-5 (paperback : alk. ppr.)

∞™ The paper used in this publication meets the minimum
requirements of American National Standard for Information
Sciences—Permanence of Paper for Printed Library Materials,
ANSI Z39.48—1984

In memory of

Margaret M. Gallagher

Jack Gallagher

and

Charles C. Forman

CONTENTS

Acknowledgments		vii
Introduction		1
Prologue	"Différent de soi-même:" the Altered Self in Balzac, Flaubert, and Zola	7
Chapter I	Flaubert's *Madame Bovary* and Mauriac's *Thérèse Desqueyroux*: Influence With No Apparent Anxiety	13
Chapter II	Gender and Sexuality	
	Displacements of the Maternal in *Madame Bovary*	29
	Sexual Ambiguity in *Thérèse Desqueyroux*	38
Chapter III	Religion and its Uses	
	The Sacraments in *Madame Bovary* and *Thérèse Desqueyroux*	47
	Monsieur Bournisien: Flaubert's *Curé de Campagne*	55
Chapter IV	Novel Uncertainties	
	Narrative Uncertainty in *Madame Bovary*	73
	"Elle se penche sur sa propre énigme:" *Thérèse Desqueyroux*, a Novel of Uncertainties	77
Chapter V	Supporting Players	
	Undiscovered Countries: the Role of Some Minor Characters in *Madame Bovary*	87

	"Aussi réelle que l'autre:" Alterity in *Thérèse Desqueyroux*	92
Chapter VI	Photo Negativity in *Madame Bovary* and *Thérèse Desqueyroux*	101
Appendix A	Response to Mary Orr	109
Appendix B	Response to Alan Raitt	111
Appendix C	Dogmatic Parody in Flaubert's *Un coeur simple*	115
Conclusion		123
Bibliography of Works Cited		127
Index of Proper Names		133

ACKNOWLEDGMENTS

I wish to thank here those who have encouraged me in my work on Flaubert and Mauriac. Conversations long ago with the late Professor Dick Admussen of Washington University in Saint Louis about these two authors piqued my interest and prompted my initial research. Ed Ahearn of Brown University and Mary Orr of the University of Exeter, the English-speaking world's *doyenne* of Flaubert studies, have been unfailingly encouraging. I am very grateful to them both. Henry Majewski, Executive Director of the Howard Foundation at Brown University, and Ted Fraser of The College of the Holy Cross urged me—and not just once!—to organize my material into monographic form. My colleagues, both past and present, in French Studies at Wheaton College (Norton, Massachusetts), by their good will and their exemplary spirit of collegiality, created and sustained an exceptionally harmonious work environment. They are Kirk Anderson and Jonathan Walsh, along with Cécile Danehy, Meg Robinson-Lutz, Jeanne Whitaker and Janet Letts. I also want to thank Myriam Houcke for her careful proof-reading of the pages which follow. Wheaton colleagues on the College's Committee on Faculty Scholarship generously responded to my requests for financial assistance for this project. I am particularly grateful to Wheaton's Provost, Susanne Woods, for her many kindnesses and for her sustained and substantial support, both moral and financial.

The editors of these journals have kindly granted permission to use materials previously published in: *Dalhousie French Studies* (1998, 2000, 2001), *French Studies Bulletin* (1986, summer and winter 1997, 1998, spring and autumn 2003), *New Zealand Journal of French Studies* (1991), *Orbis Litterarum (1998)*, *Romance Languages Annual (2000)*, *Romance Notes (1986, 2003)*. Permission to reproduce passages from François Mauriac's *Thérèse Desqueyroux* has been granted by Editions Bernard Grasset, Paris.

Providence, Rhode Island
17 December 2004
In festam Sancti Lazari

INTRODUCTION

The idea for a comparative study of different aspects of Flaubert's *Madame Bovary* and Mauriac's *Thérèse Desqueyroux* first took shape as I mulled over an idea I had while teaching a course which included several novels of the nineteenth century. Besides *Madame Bovary*, these were Balzac's *Le père Goriot* and Zola's *L'Assommoir*. As I tried to construct a context in which to place an identical, pivotal scene which I found in each of these three novels, I recalled other works, both earlier and later, in which the main character also undergoes a metamorphosis of the self, albeit of a somewhat different kind, yet no less profound and life-transforming than the changes experienced by Eugène de Rastignac, by Emma Bovary, and by Gervaise Coupeau (née Macquart).

In the prologue which follows, "'Différent de soi-Même:' the Altered Self in Balzac, Flaubert, and Zola," I consider not only the three nineteenth-century scenes describing a no longer recognizable earlier self, but I also take note of another modern novel which I had at times casually thought of as like *Madame Bovary*, but without delving very deeply at all into the question of their relationship beyond formulating some vague impressions about the most obvious similarities. Long before that time in some now forgotten source, I must have come across a passing, yet apt, description of Thérèse Desqueyroux as a "modern-day Madame Bovary." Each title character is an unhappily married woman, prevented by social and economic forces from freeing herself from her tightly circumscribed, provincial life.

While considering the profound change Emma undergoes because of her visit to the château at La Vaubyessard and her transformation there into a new woman, distinctly different from the Emma Rouault of Les Bertaux, the Norman farm where she had grown up, I realized that Thérèse too has two personalities, experienced, not consecutively like Emma, but concurrently. Thérèse's bifurcated self offers some clues to explaining her highly enigmatic personality; just as Emma's newly constituted self, characterized by her self-indulgent *bovarysme*, accounts for much of her behavior after her stay at La Vaubyessard.

Rereading both novels a number of times after establishing this initial key connection, I was constantly amazed at the numerous other similarities I began to see between these two women characters. In my first chapter, "*Madame Bovary* and *Thérèse Desqueyroux*: Influence with No Apparent Anxiety," I set forth the remarkable resemblances in plot, character, and theme between Flaubert's 1857 and Mauriac's 1927 novel, resemblances which cannot convincingly be explained simply as accidental or unconscious.

A colleague, after reading that chapter, then asked me: well, what about the differences? It was a fair question, and a good one, but not an easy one to answer. The most obvious response and a reasonable one, I think, is that Mauriac took what he liked and left the rest, that he made Thérèse and her story his own, despite all the inspiration he must have found in Flaubert. The differences are, of course, manifest, yet, I would contend, less telling than the similarities. In fact, seeming differences at times evaporate when further considered.

The education of each of the title characters, for instance, appears at first glance to offer a distinct and significant difference between the heroines. The persistent, deleterious effect on Emma of her convent education, especially the dual influences of religious enthusiasm and romantic yearnings inspired by her reading of novels, constitutes a major thematic strand of Flaubert's novel. Thérèse, on the other hand, studied at a secular *lycée* and was not, like her friend Anne de la Trave, "élevée au Sacré-Coeur." And yet the reader is fairly certain that a Thérèse *au Sacré-Coeur* or an Emma *au lycée* would still have turned out being Thérèse and Emma. Charles Bovary's secular education seems to have done for him little more than what Thérèse says the nuns did for Anne: "Les dame du Sacré-coeur interposaient mille voiles entre le réel et leurs petites filles" (26).[1] Both Charles and Emma lead lives singularly out of touch with reality. So, even though the educations which Charles and Emma received were as different as the educations of Thérèse and of Anne, the personalities of the Bovarys seem formed by other forces as well—Charles's parents (especially his mother), Emma's life at Les Bertaux. In the same way, Thérèse and Anne are each products of a personal determinism, an individual and unique reaction to life in the bosom of their landed, bourgeois families.

I did, of course, take my colleague's query seriously and looked at some significant differences and their role in the two novels. Chapter 2 on the critical issues of gender and sexuality is divided into two parts: "Displacements of the Maternal in *Madame Bovary*" and "Sexual Ambiguity in *Thérèse Desqueyroux*," and examines, along with the ever-present and unavoidable similarities, highly significant differences between Emma, who at times treats as children all the men with whom she is involved sexually, and Thérèse whose sexuality emerges, upon close textual analysis, as, in all likelihood, homosexually oriented.

Both Flaubert, the non-believer, and Mauriac, the Jansenist-leaning Catholic, incorporate into their characters' lives the ceremonies of the Roman Catholic Church. Chapter 3 looks at "Religion and its Uses." In the section on "The Sacraments," it becomes clear that these rites do not prove to be terribly efficacious for either woman, yet each author's use of these cultural commonplaces of French provincial life serves a similar purpose: to show yet more disappointment in each heroine's search for solace. Emma's failure to find *félicité*, *passion*, or *ivresse* in her relationships with Charles or with her lovers, Rodolphe and Léon, leads her to more ethereal yearnings for union with the divine in an apotheosis of incorporeal love. Mauriac admits in the preface to his novel that he would have liked to see a converted Thérèse, but he stopped short of allowing her a spiritual change for fear of scandalizing the pious among his readers. His decision to resist a facile dénouement also makes for a much better novel, whose open ending haunts most readers long after the reading is over and they have put the novel down.

I have devoted a long section in this chapter on religion to the curate in Flaubert's novel. Monsieur Bournisien plays a crucial role in the life of the village and in Emma's life. His "bêtise" both drives Emma further into adultery and allows Flaubert to give free vent to his anti-clericalism. Along with the self-satisfied, bourgeois Homais, himself the object of much critical study, Bournisien, often ignored by critics, offers a perfect target for the author's ridicule; here, a searing satire of the rural clergy.

Uncertainty permeates each novel, and, as I demonstrate in Chapter 4 "Novel Uncertainties," one encounters a related sort of uncertainty in each. While Flaubert underscores the unknowability of his characters and especially the mystery of their motivations narratologically by employing a technique which supplies the title for the first section "Narrative Uncertainty in *Madame Bovary*," Mauriac creates a heroine whose personality and motivations remain maddeningly unclear. The enigma that is Thérèse exists for the reader largely because of the preponderance of uncertainty as a major thematic element in the novel, which I discuss in the second part of Chapter 4 "'Elle se penche sur sa propre énigme:' *Thérèse Desqueyroux*, a Novel of Uncertainties."

A study of some minor characters in Chapter 5 "Supporting Players" reveals their connection to the two eponymous heroines. The section on Flaubert's novel entitled "Undiscovered Countries" explores the tantalizingly limited contours the author gives us of these minor characters' lives. Several essentially undeveloped characters like the *perruquier* of Tostes and Madame Homais are other Emmas, while Justin behaves like another Charles. Mauriac, rather, surrounds Thérèse with a clan of relatives and acquaintances, all of whom, while representing some aspect of the complicated mix of her desires, embody, each one of them individually, traits which by their contrariety underscore the incompatibility of the two halves of Thérèse's split personality. I examine the role of these "others" and their relationship with Thérèse in the second part of Chapter 5, "'Aussi réelle que l'autre:' Alterity in *Thérèse Desqueyroux*."

The final Chapter 6 on "Photo Negativity" focuses on more details in each novel—in this case, the use of portraits and photographs—in order to underscore again the richness of similarities in these two fictional works.

Preceding a brief conclusion, I offer three appendices. The wealth of detail, in *Madame Bovary* especially, offers a seemingly inexhaustible source for critical comment. A friend said, upon seeing me after I had sent him the last of three essays on Flaubert's masterpiece: "You've certainly been mining Flaubert!" For the longest time, I remembered the remark differently, as more sardonic: "You've certainly been milking Flaubert!" Whether I was mining or milking, most careful readers discover a cache of subtly interconnected ideas, images, themes, and motifs in Flaubert's exquisitely crafted novel. The Flaubertian mine has a mother-lode running deep and wide and *Madame Bovary* is indeed a most fecund bovine. Appendix A is a response to Mary Orr's excellent, short study of *bovarysme* and the La Vaubyessard episode. After reading Alan Raitt's carefully constructed article on "Emma's Lost Brother," I was prompted to respond and to express some reservations about his conclusion. That response is in Appendix B. The longer Appendix C, "Dogmatic Parody in *Un coeur simple*," along with the section in Chapter 3 on Bournisien, form the two panel of a diptych. Flaubert, as I read him in his 1877 short story, again pours out his parodic bile, not against the rural clergy as in *Madame Bovary*, but against a central tenet of Roman Catholic orthodoxy: the doctrine of Eucharistic transubstantiation. Thérèse's reaction at Mass following Clara's death intimates more obliquely her own seeming abandonment of faith in the same belief. Likewise, Emma's vision at the moment of her death of the blind beggar whose "face hideuse ... se dressait dans les ténèbres éternelles comme un épouvantement " (418)[2] is surely a precursor to the author's dénouement, often read as entirely benign, in *Un coeur simple*, of twenty years later, wherein he describes the final vision of the servant Félicité in these words: "elle crut voir, dans les cieux entrouverts, un perroquet gigantesque, planant audessus de sa tête" (87).

At the beginning of his recent study *"Indiana* and *Madame Bovary*: Intertextual Echoes," John T. Booker invokes Matei Calinescu's contention that "there are texts which *haunt* each other."[3] Then having elucidated parallels and noted obvious differences in the seduction scenes in these novels by Sand and Flaubert, Booker concludes by observing that after such a reading "the reader is sure to see *both* [texts] in a new, better light" (232). My examination of and my reflections on *Madame Bovary* and *Thérèse Desqueyroux* in tandem have certainly lead me to a much better appreciation and, I hope, a better understanding of each novel. As I reread the two and thought of them together, related elements in each novel illuminated the meaning of the other work. In his May 2, 1977 *New Yorker* story "The Kugelmass Episode," Woody Allen comments mordantly on the facile dicta of literary critics. In spite of its obvious derisive intent, this observation contains some truth: "Well, I guess the mark of a classic is that you can reread it a thousand times and always find something new" (37). All the more true here when dealing with two classics. And two classics which, curiously, are rarely seen as related.

In the recently-published *A Gustave Flaubert Encyclopedia*, one finds a number of entries of authors, both French and foreign, whose work bears witness to the influence of *Madame Bovary*.[4] The writings of no fewer than eleven novelists are cited as indebted to *Madame Bovary* for their inspiration. These are: Clarín's *La Regenta* (1884-1885); Kate Chopin's *Awakening* (1889); Faulkner's *Sanctuary* (1931) and the posthumous *Flags in the Dust* (1973); several short stories by Mavis Gallant; the Austrian Elfriede Jelinek's *Lust* ("Desire," 1989); Sinclair Lewis's *Main Street* (1920); Somerset Maugham's *Mrs. Craddock* (1902), *The Painted Veil* (1925), and *The Razor's Edge* (1944); Maupassant's *Une Vie* (1883); Pardo Bazán's *El Cisne de Vila morte* (1885); Eça de Queinós's *O primo Bazilio: Episodio domestico* (1878); and, finally, the Italian

Giovanni Verga's *Il Marito di Elena* (1882). Not a word, in this list of at times obscure authors, not one word about Mauriac and *Thérèse Desqueyroux*.[5]

The pages which follow will demonstrate that François Mauriac belongs on the list as a writer whose major novel constitutes at once a unique, individual literary creation and an *hommage* to Flaubert, the master and precursor, from whom Mauriac surely drew for inspiration.

NOTES

1. François Mauriac, *Thérèse Desqueyroux*, edited by Jean Collignon, Macmillan French Literature Series (New York: Macmillan, 1963). All quotes from the novel will be from this edition. Permission to quote from Mauriac's novel has been granted by Editions Bernard Grasset.
2. Gustave Flaubert, *Madame Bovary* (Paris: Folio, 1972). All quotes from the novel will be from this edition.
3. Matei Calinescu, *Rereading* (New Haven: Yale U. P., 1993), xi, quoted in John T. Booker, "*Indiana* and *Madame Bovary*: Intertextual Echoes," *Nineteenth-Century French Studies* 31, nos. 3 & 4 (2003): 226.
4. *A Gustave Flaubert Encyclopedia*, ed. Laurence M. Porter (Westport, Ct.: Greenwood Press, 2001). For each author cited by me, see the entry listed alphabetically in the *Encyclopedia*, except that Clarín is not listed under his pseudonym but under his family name of Alas.
5. Likewise, *Gustave Flaubert's Madame Bovary: A Reference Guide*, ed. Laurence M. Porter and Eugene F. Gray (Westport, Ct.: Greenwood Press, 2002) makes no mention of Mauriac or of *Thérèse Desqueyroux*.

PROLOGUE

"Différent de soi-même:" the Altered Self in Balzac, Flaubert, and Zola

When he writes: "On est quelquefois aussi différent de soi-même que des autres"[1] La Rochefoucauld seems to underscore the frequency of these metamorphoses of the self and, indeed, one finds in major works of the late seventeenth century repeated occurrences of the failure to recognize the self. In her first scene on stage (Act I, iv), intent upon dying in order to take the secret of her incestuous passion to the grave, yet overcome with desire for her step-son, the hunter Hippolyte, Phèdre asks:

> Dieux: que ne suis-je assise à l'ombre des forêts:
> Quand pourrai-je, au travers d'une noble poussière,
> Suivre de l'œil un char fuyant dans la carrière?[2]

Her confidante Oenone, perplexed, exclaims: "Quoi, Madame?" To which Racine's heroine, jolted from her lascivious reverie, responds:

> Insensée, où suis-je? et qu'ai-je dit?
> Où laissé-je égarer mes vœux et mon esprit?
> Je l'ai perdu: les Dieux m'en ont ravi l'usage. (179-181)

Again, in Act IV, vi, by now aware of the politically dangerous love between Hippolyte and Aricie, Phèdre cuts short her diatribe against the young lovers with this realization:

> Que fais-je? Où ma raison se va-t-elle égarer?

> Moi jalouse! et Thésée est celui que j'implore!
> Mon époux est vivant, et moi je brûle encore:
> Pour qui? Quel est le cœur où prétendent mes vœux?
> Chaque mot sur mon front fait dresser mes cheveux.
> (1264-1268)

The virtuous Princesse de Clèves reacts similarly a number of times in the course of her rarefied affair with Nemours. Perhaps the most striking example occurs after the letter-writing scene during which she and Nemours—her husband, present, but narratively eclipsed—attempt to reconstruct the incriminating letter, once thought by the princess to have been addressed to Nemours, but now known to have been written to her kinsman the Vidame de Chartres. She recalls how she had treated Nemours when she still though him the addressee:

> Quand elle pensait qu'elle s'était reproché comme un crime, le jour précédent, de lui avoir donné des marques de sensibilité que la seule compassion pouvait avoir fait naître et que, par son aigreur, elle lui avait fait paraître des sentiments de jalousie qui étaient des preuves certaines de passion, elle ne se reconnaissait plus elle-même.[3]

Marked schizophrenic or split personalities, rather than passing deviations from an enduring self, are more likely in twentieth-century works. Thérèse Desqueyroux in the final chapter of Mauriac's most celebrated novel, to cite but one example, in a moment of rare lucidity and genuine insight speaks of the two distinct, irreconcilable, yet undeniable sides of her personality:

> —Mais, maintenant, Bernard, je sens bien que la Thérèse qui, d'instinct, écrase sa cigarette parce qu'un rien suffit à mettre le feu aux brandes, —la Thérèse qui aimait compter ses pins elle-même, régler ses gemmes; —la Thérèse qui était fière d'épouser un Desqueyroux, de tenir son rang au sein d'une bonne famille de la lande, contente enfin de se caser, comme on dit, cette Thérèse-là est aussi réelle que l'autre, aussi vivante; non, non: il n'y avait aucune raison de la sacrifier à l'autre. (112-113)

In three major nineteenth-century novels, there are scenes, strikingly similar to one another, in which the novel's major character becomes aware, not of a momentary deviation nor of the co-existence of two distinct and contrary parts of the self, but rather of a total transformation marked by a subsequent acknowledgment of the difference between the old and the new self. A new Adam, so to speak, has developed without however any of the self-will typical of such a change in, for example, a Gidean *Immoraliste*. Also striking is the cinematographic quality of these nineteenth-century scenes in which the transformed characters actually see themselves as they once were and barely recognize their old selves, so utterly different and distinct were they from the new.

The dual nature of Balzac's Eugène de Rastignac has not eluded critics, so clearly is the duality established and set forth by the author.[4] Yet a lengthy study of the subject fails to give any special attention to the pivotal scene in which the protagonist himself becomes aware of the change from the old self to the new:

> Jusqu'alors il n'avait même pas complètement secoué le charme des fraîches et suaves idées qui enveloppent comme d'un feuillage la jeunesse des enfants élevés en province. Il avait continuellement hésité à franchir le Rubicon parisien.... Néanmoins ses derniers scrupules avaient disparu la veille, quand il s'était vu dans son appartement ... il avait dépouillé sa peau d'homme de province, et s'était doucement établi dans une position d'où il découvrait un bel avenir. Aussi, en attendant Delphine, mollement assis dans ce joli boudoir qui devenait un peu le sien, se voyait-il si loin du Rastignac venu l'année dernière à Paris, qu'en le lorgnant par un effet d'optique morale, il se demandait s'il se ressemblait en ce moment à lui-même.[5]

Flaubert's Madame Bovary takes a similar look at her old self during the dinner scene at La Vaubyessard:

> L'air du bal était lourd; les lampes pâlissaient. On refluait dans la salle de billard. Un domestique monta sur une chaise et cassa deux vitres; au bruit des éclats de verre, Mme Bovary tourna la tête et aperçut dans le jardin, contre les carreaux, des faces de paysans qui regardaient. Alors le souvenir des Bertaux lui arriva. Elle revit la ferme, la mare bourbeuse, son père en blouse sous les pommiers, et elle se revit elle-même, comme autrefois, écrémant avec son doigt les terrines de lait dans la laiterie. Mais, aux fulgurations de l'heure présente, sa vie passée, si nette jusqu'alors, s'évanouissait tout entière, et elle doutait presque de l'avoir vécue. (83)

And finally Gervaise Coupeau (née Macquart), the proletarian heroine of Zola's *L'Assommoir*, realizes how she has changed (and for the worse) while all around her has remained essentially the same, as she sees herself as she had been, ebulliently optimistic, thirteen years before:

> Ah! non, la vie ne tournait pas gentiment, ce n'était guère l'existence qu'elle avait espérée. Au lieu d'avoir des fleurs sur sa vieillesse, elle roulait dans les choses qui ne sont pas propres. Un jour, se penchant, elle eut une drôle de sensation, elle crut se voir en personne là-bas, sous le porche, près de la loge du concierge, le nez en l'air, examinant la maison pour la première fois; et ce saut de treize ans en arrière lui donna un élancement au cœur. La cour n'avait pas changé ... même, dans le coin humide de la fontaine, une mare coulée de la teinturerie avait une belle teinte bleue, d'un bleu aussi tendre que le bleu de jadis. Mais elle, à cette heure, se sentait joliment changée et décatie. Elle n'était plus en bas, d'abord, la figure vers le ciel, contente et

courageuse, ambitionnant un bel appartement. Elle était sous les toits, dans le coin des pouilleux, dans le trou le plus sale, à l'endroit où l'on ne recevait jamais la visite d'un rayon.[6]

It seems less important to try to prove whether these isolated passages are to be explained as textual borrowings, as examples of unconscious influence, or simply as accidental similarities in a sub-genre like the *Bildungsroman*. What is striking is that each one of France's three great novelists of the nineteenth century chose to convey the reality of the altered self in essentially the same fashion, and more remarkable still used for this an undeniably modern technique, and cinematographic *avant la lettre*, for each epiphanic scene contains a literary equivalent of the cinematic flashback; and, indeed, a very specialized type of flashback, in which the major characters all see themselves as they once were, but are no more.[7]

Unlike the three nineteenth-century examples just explored which share one common scene, we will see that Flaubert's novel and Mauriac's share so many similarities that, in the final analysis, these similarities cannot simply, reasonably, or convincingly be explained away as merely accidental.

In the pages which follow it will become clear that, while different from Emma Bovary, Thérèse Desqueyroux, a tormented woman who struggles without success to reconcile a split personality, will also, like the three nineteenth-century characters just described, think of herself as she was or as she might have been or might be. Mauriac's own cinematic-like flashbacks fill not merely the first eight chapters of his novel, but recur again and again in its final chapters as his heroine uses memories and imaginings both to contrast her past and her present and to decide how to act when the present seems eerily to resemble the past. But the resemblances between Emma Bovary and Thérèse Desqueyroux go far beyond the question of self-recognition. In many ways, as we shall see, Thérèse Desqueyroux is, indeed, as some now-forgotten source once suggested, a modern-day Madame Bovary. This contention is not simply a facile metonymy but the admission of a remarkable sisterly identity.

NOTES

1. La Rochefoucauld, François de, *Maximes*, ed. J. Truchet (Paris: Garnier, 1967), 36. This maxim, number 135, in earlier versions and in a somewhat different formulation in the Liancourt MS and the Holland edition contained the temporal *souvent* not *quelquefois* (see pp. 420 and 450).

2. J. Racine, *Phèdre* (Paris: Petits Classiques Bordas, 1970), vv. 176-178.

3. Madame de Lafayette, *La Princesse de Clèves* (Paris: Garnier-Flammarion, 1966), 118.
4. Trevor Field, "The Split Personality of Eugène de Rastignac," *Romance Studies* 5 (1984): 167-81.
5. H. de Balzac, *Le père Goriot* (Paris: Garnier-Flammarion, 1966), 203.
6. E. Zola, *L'Assommoir*, vol. 2 of *Les Rougon-Macquart* (Paris: Bibliothèque de la Pléiade, 1961), 673.
7. James Monaco in his *How to Read a Film* (New York: Oxford U. P., 1977), 408, defines flashback as "a scene that is inserted into a scene in 'present' time and that deals with the past."

CHAPTER I

Flaubert's *Madame Bovary* and Mauriac's *Thérèse Desqueyroux*: Influence With No Apparent Anxiety[1]

While it is perhaps easier to state what it is that Emma Bovary and Thérèse Desqueyroux do not have in common than to list all the many similarities between these two remarkable, female title characters, the sheer number and importance of the similarities must strike readers as nothing less than startling.[2] Such a preponderance of parallelisms is surely worthy of study and cannot be attributed simply to happenstance, nor, can one agree with the contention that "... Mauriac a dû, inconsciemment peut-être et à son insu, s'inspirer du modèle littéraire de *Madame Bovary*."[3]

Several times in his writings, Mauriac appropriated a Flaubertian trope to discuss his own relationship with his eponymous heroine, Thérèse. In 1962, Mauriac, commenting on his celebrated fictional character, after seeing Georges Franju's film *Thérèse Desqueyroux*, wrote in his *Bloc-notes*: "Thérèse devait être une image brouillée de mes propres complications, j'imagine. Mme Bovary, c'est toujours nous."[4] Cecil Jenkins in his 1965 book-length study of Mauriac, without stating the source, quotes the author who had declared: "Thérèse Desqueyroux was myself."[5] Surprisingly, or perhaps because it is so obvious, he fails to mention the Flaubertian echo in Mauriac's formulation. In 1976, referring evidently to the same quote, Robert Speaight furnishes the context, but not the precise source: "When Mauriac was asked whether he could say, as Flaubert had said of Madame Bovary: 'Thérèse Desqueyroux—c'est moi,' he admitted that she was 'made up of everything that in myself I have been obliged to overcome, or circumvent, or ignore.'"[6]

The germ from which each novel sprang or the fillip which inspired each novelist to begin constructing his plot was an incident involving a real, provincial married woman and a contemporary of the author. The briefest summary of the Delamare affair suffices to suggest how this *fait divers* served as an inspiration for Flaubert's celebrated "roman sur rien:"

> Un ancien élève de son père, Delamare, médecin de Ry, avait épousé en secondes noces une femme qui, après l'avoir trompé, s'était empoisonnée. Delamare en était mort de chagrin.[7]

Mauriac had himself attended the trial of Madame Canaby, the accused, but later exonerated, poisoner of her feckless husband. Jean Lacouture has written about the effect of this famous 1905 trial on the novelist: "Surgie informe de ses propres abîmes, Thérèse a pris là corps et visage. L'affaire Canaby lui a fourni une face et une silhouette."[8]

The major lines of each novel are undeniably the same: a young, provincial woman marries the wrong man for the wrong reasons, almost immediately becomes profoundly unhappy, seeks and may find solace with other men, imagines ideal lovers, turns to religion for consolation, demonstrates an utter lack of affection for her daughter, twice contemplates suicide, and finally gains release.

Even very superficial resemblances are apparent: each heroine's name, not only before but also after marriage, resonates with the other, containing as each does an identical number of syllables. Emma Rouault and Thérèse Larroque become Emma Bovary and Thérèse Desqueyroux.

While from different social classes—Emma is the only surviving child of a prosperous, widowed, Norman farmer; Thérèse, the only daughter of a timber-rich and politically-ambitious widower from les Landes—each will find herself the target within her new family of a relentlessly critical mother-in-law. Madame Bovary *mère* can abide neither Emma's spendthrift ways nor her suspect reading habits; Madame de la Trave sees Thérèse as deliberately paradoxical and, worse, unforgivably unmaternal. Emma is "une insolente! une évaporée! pire, peut-être!" (256); as for Thérèse, "On savait déjà qu'il y avait des gens capables d'assassiner ... mais c'est son hypocrisie! Ça, c'est épouvantable!" (102).

Emma marries Charles, thinking she loves him, having mistaken the excitement of a male presence for the tingling of passion, but also to free herself from the tedium of farm life, for helping her father at Les Bertaux bores her terribly:

> Mais l'anxiété d'un état nouveau, ou peut-être l'irritation causée par la présence de cet homme, avait suffi à lui faire croire qu'elle possédait enfin cette passion merveilleuse qui jusqu'alors s'était tenue comme un grand oiseau au plumage rose planant dans la splendeur des ciels poétiques; —et elle ne pouvait s'imaginer à présent que ce calme où elle vivait fût le bonheur qu'elle avait rêvé. (68)

Thérèse, no less practical, but less emotional, seeks protection from a vaguely perceived threat by taking refuge through matrimony in the Desqueyroux family:

> ... elle voulait être rassurée contre elle ne savait quel péril ... elle s'incrustait dans un bloc familial, "elle se casait"; elle entrait dans un ordre. Elle se sauvait. (33)

Each young woman is terribly mismatched, having married an emotionally and intellectually lesser person than herself. The mediocre and plodding Charles is no knight-errant like those Emma had read about so often in romantic novels:

> Elle aurait voulu vivre dans quelque vieux manoir, comme ces châtelaines ... qui ... passaient leurs jours ... à regarder venir du fond de la campagne un cavalier à plume blanche qui galope sur un cheval noir. (64-65)

For the intellectually curious Thérèse, Bernard incarnates both bourgeois conformity and religious hypocrisy. Each *mal mariée* exclaims her misery with a chillingly similar phraseology. Emma laments:

> —Pourquoi, mon Dieu! me suis-je mariée? (74)

For Thérèse the question is:

> Pourquoi l'avait-elle épousé? (32)

No later than on her honeymoon, Thérèse is so disgusted by what she considers Bernard's sexual depravity that she wishes she could push him from their conjugal bed into the void:

> D'une main brutale et qui pourtant ne l'éveilla pas, de nouveau elle l'écarta.... Ah! l'écarter une fois pour toutes et à jamais! le précipiter hors du lit, dans les ténèbres. (44)

Early in her affair with Rodolphe, when the lovers' nocturnal trysts occur only after Charles falls asleep, Emma too wants desperately to be rid of Charles: "Elle se dévorait d'impatience; si ses yeux l'avaient pu, ils l'eussent fait sauter par la fenêtre" (227). Later, Emma simply takes herself to a separate bedroom in order to be alone and free of Charles's presence which she finds importunate and insufferable.

Emblematic of the estrangement of each woman from her husband is a scene in each novel detailing the interposition between the couple of another character. During the newly-weds' first days in Yonville, as Emma's romantic interest in the young clerk Léon grows, Flaubert describes how a typical evening at the Bovarys' begins:

> M. Homais arrivait pendant le dîner.... Puis, quand il s'était posé à sa place, contre la table, entre les deux époux, il demandait au médecin des nouvelles de ses malades.... (139)

Mauriac presents the same literal separation of the Desqueyroux at the very moment the couple are reunited after Thérèse's acquittal and upon her return to Argelouse:

> Bernard aida la tante à grimper dans la carriole, et prit les rênes.... Tante Clara s'assit entre les époux. Il fallait lui crier dans l'oreille que tout était arrangé.... (79)

Utter lack of communication with or incomprehension by their spouses and families greatly demoralizes each woman. Thérèse, in the midst of the Desqueyroux family, cannot blame their hostility and inability to understand her on willful decisions on their part. She admits, rather, that communication between her and them is simply not possible:

> C'était là le tragique: qu'il n'y eût pas une raison de rupture: l'événement était impossible à prévoir qui aurait empêché les choses d'aller leur train jusqu'à la mort. La mésentente suppose un terrain de rencontre où se heurter; mais Thérèse ne rencontrait jamais Bernard, et moins encore ses beaux-parents.... Avaient-ils seulement un vocabulaire commun? Ils donnaient aux mots essentiels un sens différent. (70-71)

From early in their marriage, Emma had vituperated against Charles and his inability to understand or even to be aware of her unhappiness:

> Si Charles l'avait voulu, cependant, s'il s'en fût douté, si son regard, une seule fois, fût venu à la rencontre de sa pensée, il lui semblait qu'une abondance subite se serait détachée de son coeur, comme tombe la récolte d'un espalier, quand on y porte la main. Mais, à mesure que se serrait davantage l'intimité de leur vie, un détachement intérieur se faisait qui la déliait de lui. (70)

Married life for each woman proves to be unbearable. On her wedding day, Thérèse feels that she "allait se confondre avec le troupeau de celles qui ont servi" (35). Later when pregnant, she feels no less dehumanized, describing herself this way:

> Les la Trave vénéraient en moi un vase sacré; le réceptacle de leur progéniture; aucun doute que, le cas échéant, ils m'eussent sacrifiée à cet embryon. Je perdais le sentiment de mon existence individuelle. (69)

So oppressive is her domestic life that her unhappiness drives her to contemplate suicide, to wish in her misery for the destruction of the man responsible for her sister-in-law's ecstatic joy, and eventually to begin the slow poisoning of her insipid spouse, Bernard. *Her* life depends on ending his:

> Elle traversait, seule, un tunnel, vertigineusement; elle en était au plus obscur; il fallait, sans réfléchir, comme une brute, sortir de ces ténèbres, de cette fumée, atteindre l'air libre, vite! vite! (75)

Emma also presents physical symptoms of conjugal unhappiness. Unlike in the story, told to Emma by her maid, of La Guérine who suffered terribly until she married, Emma's malady dates, in fact, from the time of her marriage to Charles. Emma's maid recounts La Guérine's illness:

> Elle était si triste, si triste, qu'à la voir debout sur le seuil de sa maison, elle vous faisait l'effet d'un drap d'enterrement tendu devant la porte. Son mal, à ce qu'il paraît, était une manière de brouillard qu'elle avait dans la tête, et les médecins n'y pouvaient rien, ni le curé non plus. (154)

To which Emma replies:

> Mais moi ... c'est après le mariage que ça m'est venu. (154)

It is not until she begins her adulterous affair with Rodolphe that Emma ever feels part of a group, the obverse, in a sense, of Thérèse's "troupeau de celles qui ont servi:"

> Alors elle se rappela les héroïnes des livres qu'elle avait lus, et la légion lyrique de ces femmes adultères se mit à chanter dans sa mémoire avec des voix de soeurs qui la charmaient. (219)

Both of these unhappily-wed women abhor the married state, each using practically the same phraseology to describe her disgust and visceral repugnance. Emma speaks of "les souillures du mariage" which sullied "la fraîcheur de sa beauté" (296). For Thérèse "cette ineffaçable salissure des noces" contrasts with "tout ce qui précède mon mariage [et qui] prend dans mon souvenir cet aspect de pureté" (25).

Each woman's profound unhappiness is often hidden from others by role-playing. Throughout the novel, at the most intense moments of her adulterous liaisons with Rodolphe and Léon, Emma always gives the impression of being the virtuous wife and mother. All the while loving Léon platonically but passionately,

> On la vit prendre à coeur son ménage, retourner à l'église régulièrement et tenir sa servante avec plus de sévérité.... Les bourgeoises admiraient son économie, les clients sa politesse, les pauvres sa charité. (150-151)

Much later, after her reconciliation with Rodolphe which follows Charles's disastrous operation on Hippolyte's club-foot, Emma assumes the same role, all the while taking delight in her daydreams about Rodolphe:

> Alors, tout en faisant l'épouse et la vertueuse, elle s'enflammait à l'idée de cette tête dont les cheveux noirs se tournaient en une boucle vers le front hâlé, de cette taille à la fois si robuste et si élégante, de cet homme enfin qui possédait tant d'expérience dans la raison, tant d'emportement dans le désir! (250)

Thérèse too plays a role or, more precisely, wears a mask to conceal her true feelings. After reading Anne's lyrical letter about her nascent passion for Jean Azévédo, Thérèse wishes Bernard was not with her: "... qu'elle n'ait plus ce souci de composer son visage, d'éteindre son regard...." (42). Just a while later, when she forgets herself, Bernard is shocked by the uncomposed face he does see:

> —Voyons, Thérèse, ne fais pas cette figure: si tu te voyais
> ....
> Elle sourit, se remasqua.... (44)

In their role-playing, Thérèse seems much more conscious of what she is doing, and, indeed, one has the clear sense that Mauriac's heroine is, in the main, more lucid than Flaubert's. In fact, the first eight chapters of *Thérèse Desqueyroux* constitute Thérèse's retrospective examination of conscience in preparation for her encounter with Bernard. Yet, despite Thérèse's frequent soul-searching, the reader is struck by her lack of candor as, for example, when she recalls the slow poisoning of Bernard. The process started "sans qu'abrutie de chaleur, Thérèse ait songé à l'avertir qu'il a doublé sa dose habituelle" (73). When he then asks if he has, in fact, taken his Fowler drops, Thérèse "s'est tue par paresse, sans doute, par fatigue.... 'Impossible que j'aie prémédité de me taire'" (73). Her recollections of what followed are always expressed in passive constructions: "... elle s'est engouffrée dans le crime béant; elle a été aspirée par le crime...."(74). All the crises of Bernard's malady are recounted as if Thérèse had played no part at all in them. She describes simply his condition, not her agency. She mentions, for example, "cette soudaine reprise de son mal" and speaks of what happened "après une crise plus alarmante" and then says that "Au début de décembre, une reprise de son mal terrassa Bernard" (74-75).

Perhaps only twice does Emma Bovary seem able to see and admit the truth of her situation. The first moment of lucidity during the opera in Rouen is, however, short-lived and quite fleeting. After thinking how happy life could have been had she met the ideal man and just before becoming enthralled by the presence of the tenor Lagardy, Emma does seem to realize the true shallowness of her existence:

> Mais ce bonheur-là, sans doute, était un mensonge imaginé pour le désespoir de tout désir. Elle connaissait à présent la petitesse des passions que l'art exagérait. S'efforçant donc d'en détourner sa pensée, Emma voulait ne plus voir dans cette reproduction de ses douleurs qu'une fantaisie plastique bonne à amuser les yeux, et même elle souriait intérieurement d'une pitié dédaigneuse.... (296)

In Rouen, on the brink of the collapse of her affair with Léon, a flash of lucidity and a vivid awareness of her true situation is again thinly sandwiched between examples of her usual illusory denial of reality. Between her recollection of the imagined calm of her student days in the convent and her recurring hope that the ideal lover hovers nearby, the narrator describes her thoughts this way:

> ... elle n'était pas heureuse, ne l'avait jamais été. D'où venait donc cette insuffisance de la vie, cette pourriture instantanée des choses où elle s'appuyait? (368)

In her own solitary youth, Thérèse had always found solace in the company of Bernard's half-sister, Anne de la Trave. Indeed, the thought of becoming Anne's sister-in-law is one of the reasons Thérèse proffers for having wanted to marry Bernard. Upon learning in a letter from Anne of Anne's infatuation with Jean Azévédo, Thérèse ritually punctures his photo with a pin, tears up the mutilated picture, and flushes the pieces down the toilet. At that moment, terribly alone, wed to Bernard, deprived of Anne's consoling companionship, Thérèse throws the torn pieces of Anne's letter from her hotel window. So distraught is she that, at this moment, she contemplates suicide for the first time:

> Elle imaginait la tache de son corps en bouillie sur la chaussée, —et alentours ce remous d'agents, de rôdeurs.... Trop d'imagination pour se tuer, Thérèse. (45)

Similarly, Emma, abandoned by Rodolphe, after reading his letter breaking off their affair and their planned flight to Italy, stands poised at the attic window on the verge of abandoning herself to the pull of gravity, only to be interrupted by Charles's call:

> Elle jetait les yeux tout autour d'elle avec l'envie que la terre croulât. Pourquoi n'en pas finir? Et elle s'avança, elle regarda les pavés en se disant: —Allons! allons! (272)

Emma had sought happiness and fulfillment in her adulterous liaison with Rodolphe, as she will later on with Léon. Yet each relationship proves to be profoundly unsatisfying. While Léon, like Charles, never succeeds in being equal to Emma's ideal lover and although, in many ways, Rodolphe appears to be a perfect incarnation of the ideal man Emma has dreamt of, from the time of her honeymoon with Charles on, no real man ever lives up to the phantom, spectral lovers who people Emma's daydreams. Consider just two examples: the first from her first days with Charles:

> Que ne pouvait-elle s'accouder sur le balcon des chalets suisses ou enfermer sa tristesse dans un cottage écossais, avec un mari vêtu d'un habit de velours noir à longues basques et qui porte des bottes molles, un chapeau pointu et des manchettes! (69)

and another from the days just before the end of her affair with Léon:

> ... elle percevait un autre homme, un fantôme fait de ses plus ardents souvenirs, de ses lectures les plus belles, de ses convoitises les plus fortes; et il devenait à la fin si véritable, et accessible, qu'elle en palpitait émerveillée, sans pouvoir néanmoins le nettement imaginer, tant il se perdait, comme un dieu, sous l'abondance de ses attributs. (376)

While Emma thought similarly of Rodolphe as "mon roi, mon idole" (254), in the end, he manages to prove in every way, and even to the unperspicacious Emma, to be neither regal nor worthy of adoration.

Thérèse too, even in the midst of her imaginings about a meeting in Paris with Azévédo, is drawn to other, less clearly conceived of companions. She refuses the attention of a young man because

> Un être était dans sa vie grâce auquel tout le reste du monde lui paraissait insignifiant ... une créature très humble, très obscure; mais toute l'existence de Thérèse tournait autour de ce soleil visible pour son seul regard, et dont sa chair seule connaissait la chaleur. Paris grondait comme le vent dans les pins. Ce corps contre son corps, aussi léger qu'il fût, l'empêchait de respirer; mais elle aimait mieux perdre le souffle que l'éloigner. (95-96)[9]

During her sequestration at Argelouse, she becomes obsessed by fragmented, spectral presences:

> Puis le décor se défaisait, devenait moins précis, et il ne restait qu'une charmille, un banc devant la mer. Thérèse, assise, reposait sa tête contre une épaule, se levait à l'appel de la cloche pour le repas, entrait dans la charmille noire et quelqu'un marchait à ses côtés qui

soudain l'entourait des deux bras, l'attirait. Un baiser, songe-t-elle, doit arrêter le temps; elle imagine qu'il existe dans l'amour des secondes infinies. (97-98)

Both of these women, so deprived of love, turn for solace to religion. Emma transposes expressions of carnal passion from her many adulterous rendez-vous to the devotional realm. Recovering from her long illness after being rejected by Rodolphe:

> Quand elle se mettait à genoux sur son prie-Dieu gothique, elle adressait au Seigneur les mêmes paroles de suavité qu'elle murmurait jadis à son amant, dans les épanchements de l'adultère. C'était pour faire venir la croyance; mais aucune délectation ne descendait des cieux, et elle se relevait, les membres fatigués, avec le sentiment vague d'une immense duperie. (284)

The luxuries Emma had permitted herself during her affair are now similarly replaced by cultic extravagances which, she hopes, may allow her to achieve not only holiness but literal sainthood:

> Elle entrevit, parmi les illusions de son espoir, un état de pureté flottant au-dessus de la terre, se confondant avec le ciel, et où elle aspira d'être. Elle voulut devenir une sainte. Elle acheta des chapelets, elle porta des amulettes; elle souhaitait avoir dans sa chambre, au chevet de sa couche, un reliquaire enchâssé d'émeraudes, pour le baiser tous les soirs. (283)

Thérèse's interest in religious belief and practice, on the other hand, is undeniably more profound. During her pregnancy she seeks out the curate's presence:

> Thérèse, pour l'entendre, fréquenta l'église.... Ah! lui, peut-être, aurait-il pu l'aider à débrouiller en elle ce monde confus; différent des autres, lui aussi avait pris un parti tragique; à sa solitude intérieure, il avait ajouté ce désert que crée la soutane autour de l'homme qui la revêt. Quel réconfort puisait-il dans ces rites quotidiens? Thérèse aurait voulu assister à sa messe dans la semaine, alors que sans autre témoin que l'enfant de choeur, il murmurait des paroles, courbé sur un morceau de pain. Mais cette démarche eût paru étrange à sa famille et aux gens du bourg, on aurait crié à la conversion. (70)

Thérèse's remarkable leap of faith as she considers self-destruction, while without further consequence, can only be judged genuine:

> S'il existe, cet Etre...; puisqu'Il existe, qu'Il détourne la main criminelle avant que ce soit trop tard; —et si c'est sa volonté qu'une

> pauvre âme aveugle franchisse le passage, puisse-t-Il, du moins, accueillir avec amour ce monstre, sa créature. (89-90)

Yet when Aunt Clara's unexpected death does cause her hand to be stayed, this just enunciated act of faith is totally forgotten: "Si on lui parlait d'une volonté particulière, elle hausserait les épaules" (90).

After her acquittal and during the desperate days of her sequestration at Argelouse, Thérèse creates imaginary scenarios in order to evade the terrible reality of her incarceration. Like Emma, she imagines herself undergoing a saintly transformation, and one which enables her to work miracles:

> On s'agenouillait autour de son grabat. Un enfant d'Argelouse (un de ceux qui fuyaient à son approche), était apporté mourant dans la chambre de Thérèse; elle posait sur lui sa main toute jaunie de nicotine, et il se relevait guéri. (97)

Neither love nor religion offers a lasting solace to these women, nor does motherhood. Emma's hopes for a son, who represents "la revanche en espoir de toutes ses impuissances passées" (128), remain unrealized. She faints upon hearing the news that she has borne a girl. Later, returning home and utterly frustrated after her fruitless confessional conversation with the curate, Monsieur Bournisien, she brutally pushes Berthe away. Then standing at the sleeping child's bedside after Charles has dressed her cut cheek, Emma makes this observation: "C'est une chose étrange, pensait Emma, comme cette enfant est laide" (162).

Thérèse's relationship with Marie is likewise strained. Like Emma, who apparently without any feeling of compunction sends her infant daughter to the most wretched of wet-nurses, Thérèse exhibits none of the maternal instincts of the other women in her family. Mauriac uses an attention getting litotes to make this point: "Le bruit commençait de courir que le sentiment maternel ne l'étouffait pas" (71). In point of fact, Thérèse, using the same distancing demonstrative adjective *cette* as Emma, sees herself as totally detached from her child: "Cette enfant n'a rien de moi, insistait-elle" (71) and "Avec cette chair détachée de la sienne, elle désirait ne plus rien posséder en commun" (71).

Mauriac shows us Thérèse, as Flaubert had presented Emma, observing her child asleep in bed. Thérèse's earlier protests that the child bore no resemblance at all to her prove to be untrue. It is precisely the profound similarity between mother and daughter which troubles Thérèse, as she visits the child before going to her own room where she intends to drink of the poison she had used unsuccessfully on Bernard:

> Thérèse reconnaît cette oreille trop grande: son oreille. Les gens ont raison; une réplique d'elle-même est là, engourdie, endormie. "Je m'en vais, —mais cette part de moi-même demeure et tout ce destin à

remplir jusqu'au bout, dont pas un iota ne sera omis." Tendances, inclinations, lois du sang, lois inéluctables. (89)

Thérèse, about to destroy herself, can well understand other criminal parents who kill their offsprings before killing themselves:

> Thérèse a lu que des désespérés emportent avec eux leurs enfants dans la mort; les bonnes gens laissent choir leur journal: comment des choses pareilles sont-elles possibles? Parce qu'elle est un monstre, Thérèse sent profondément que cela est possible et que pour un rien.... (89)

Emma and Thérèse forfeit their maternal roles and seek too, at all costs, to break out of their traditional domestic roles. Emma yearns for the freedom men have and of which women are deprived. She laments:

> Mais une femme est empêchée continuellement. Inerte et flexible à la fois, elle a contre elle les mollesses de la chair avec les dépendances de la loi. Sa volonté, comme le voile de son chapeau retenu par un cordon, palpite à tous les vents, il y a toujours quelque désir qui entraîne, quelque convenance qui retient. (128)

Later at the Comices Agricoles with Rodolphe, she will counter his complaints about what is lacking in his life by citing advantages she covets: "... vous êtes libre ... riche" (191).

Emma makes manifest her envy of masculine freedom when, throughout the novel, she appropriates for herself male modes of dress and behavior; consider, for example:

> Ses regards devinrent plus hardis, ses discours plus libres; elle eut même l'inconvenance de se promener avec M. Rodolphe une cigarette à la bouche, *comme pour narguer le monde*; enfin, ceux qui doutaient encore ne doutèrent plus quand on la vit, un jour, descendre de *l'Hirondelle*, la taille serrée dans un gilet, à la façon d'un homme.... (255)

Dacia Maraini correctly observes, while commenting on this very passage, that these small rebellions against the constraints on those of her sex are simply symbolic and in no way indicative of any will to overthrow traditional gender roles: "... we are still, Flaubert seems to tell us, only in the realm of mere trickery. This elaborate game of switching genders ends with the gratuitous assertion of an empty gesture."[10]

Despite or, perhaps, because of her father's simplistic opinion about women—toutes des hystériques quand elles ne sont pas idiotes! (55)—Thérèse feels terribly threatened by the cruel repression of her individuality orchestrated by her husband's family :

> ... elle n'avait pas détruit cette famille, c'était elle qui serait donc détruite ... ils allaient, avec une lente méthode, l'anéantir. "Contre moi, désormais, cette puissante mécanique familiale sera montée...."
> (87)

And little wonder, since her grandmother Julie Bellade had been expunged from the collective familial memory and from the picture albums too, apparently for some unspecified offense of female self-assertion. (There will be more about these acts of the symbolic extirpation of individualists from the Desqueyroux family in Chapter 6).

Thérèse, like Emma, manifests male traits in reaction to the stifling *mores* of provincial society. She, like the men in her family, has a sense of property in her blood:

> ... rien ne vaut de vivre que de posséder la terre. Mais faut-il faire ou non la part du feu? Et si l'on s'y résigne, dans quelle mesure? Thérèse, "qui avait la propriété dans le sang", eût voulu qu'avec ce cynisme la question fût posée, mais elle haïssait les faux semblants dont les Larroque et les la Trave masquaient leur commune passion.
> (56)

Emma always fails in love and then, as a result of her irresponsible profligacy, brings financial ruin upon herself and Charles. While she succeeded in her campaign to have conferred on her a male financial role, at every turn the power of attorney granted her by a complacent and trusting Charles is used by Emma selfishly and irresponsibly and, in the end, to the utter detriment of her family. Desperate and unable to raise any of the 8,000 francs owed her creditors, Emma poisons herself with arsenic taken from Homais' capharnaüm. Assuming the role, quite familiar to her from her readings, of the doomed romantic heroine, she consumes the poison and immediately feels a sense of peace as she returns home to die: "... apaisée, et presque dans la sérénité d'un devoir accompli" (405). Imagining that death will come like sleep, she and the reader will soon be disabused of their romantic notions as Emma suffers prolonged and quite horrible death throes described in clinical detail by the narrator.

Thérèse, to escape Bernard's sentence of life-long sequestration at Argelouse, decides to take the very poison she had used to try to kill him. She, however, finds this act harder to accomplish than does Emma, for Thérèse is not sure that death will bring a peaceful void:

> Thérèse n'est pas assurée du néant. Thérèse n'est pas absolument sûre qu'il n'y ait personne. Thérèse se hait de ressentir une telle terreur. Elle qui n'hésitait pas à y précipiter autrui se cabre devant le néant. Que sa lâcheté l'humilie! (89)

And while Emma succeeds in destroying herself, Thérèse's act is interrupted, she survives, and is not again tempted to end her life, at least not actively, although her listless self-abandonment during her subsequent sequestration at Argelouse may well constitute a passive act of attempted self-destruction.

Before resorting to this ultimate solution, Emma had often dreamt of escaping her insufferable domestic situation: to Paris when she imagined the Vicomte there, to Italy with Rodolphe, into a life of artistic elegance as Lagardy's mistress. Yet, her only successful escape is to the faded splendor of the Hôtel de Boulogne in nearby Rouen to a room rented for her hebdomadal sexual encounters with Léon. Even this escape from Charles and the quotidian ennui of Yonville proves unsatisfying, and, in the end, unsustainable. Even in her final escape into death, Emma will be denied a sense of calm release. Just as dying proves for her to be much more painful than simply falling asleep, so the consoling idea of the peace of the grave is shattered, as she is about to expire, by the appearance below her bedroom window of the blind man whose hideously deformed face, so often seen by her upon leaving her lover each Thursday in Rouen, now comes to represent for her what awaits her in the beyond:

> Et Emma se mit à rire, d'un rire atroce, frénétique, désespéré, croyant voir la face hideuse du misérable, qui se dressait dans les ténèbres éternelles comme un épouvantement. (418)

Thérèse fortuitously escapes death, interrupted by the news of Clara's sudden and unexpected demise. Unlike Emma, then, Thérèse, it seems, will be able to achieve her hoped-for independence and freedom away from Bernard and the suffocating atmosphere of provincial life. She will be set free by Bernard, allowed to settle in Paris, supported by the income from their pine forests. Yet like Emma's death which holds for Flaubert's title character no yearned-for surcease, Thérèse's move to the capital and away from Bernard and the oppression of the family will prove unsatisfying too, for a part of Thérèse loves and wants to remain connected with the surroundings she must now leave and even with the family which had so stifled her personality. If Emma Bovary typifies an unreconstructed romantic soul, Thérèse exhibits an irreconcilably split personality, for at the end of the novel: "Si Bernard lui avait dit: 'Je te pardonne; viens ...', elle se serait levée, l'aurait suivi" (114). And this is so, because a part of Thérèse wants desperately to be at Argelouse in the bosom of this family. The dramatic declaration of her irreconcilable, dual nature is worth citing here in full:

> —Mais, maintenant, Bernard, je sens bien que la Thérèse qui, d'instinct, écrase sa cigarette parce qu'un rien suffit à mettre le feu aux brandes, —la Thérèse qui aimait compter ses pins elle-même, régler ses gemmes; —la Thérèse qui était fière d'épouser un Desqueyroux, de tenir son rang au sein d'une bonne famille de la lande, contente enfin de se caser, comme on dit, cette Thérèse-là est aussi réelle

> que l'autre, aussi vivante; non, non; il n'y avait aucune raison de la
> sacrifier à l'autre.
> —Quelle autre?
> Elle ne sut que répondre.... (112-113)

Generations of women in these provincial French families all seem to suffer dire fates. We know nothing of Emma's mother except that, at her death, Emma had someone make a funeral tableau from the dead woman's hair. Emma's mother, although she died while Emma was at school in the convent of the Ursulines of Rouen, seems to have left little trace in her daughter's life. Emma's premature death will have a greater effect on Berthe. Destitute and orphaned, she is sent, in the final paragraphs of the novel, to earn her living in a cotton mill. If she survives to adulthood, the family name will either be lost when she marries, or die out at her death. As it will, too, even if the unnamed aunt who looks after Berthe is also a Bovary (see Appendix B).

The loss of the family name is key when Bernard, during their last conversation in Paris, tells Thérèse that it is not the bachelor's life he will henceforth live, separated from her, that he regrets, but rather: "Je regrette seulement que nous ayons eu une fille; à cause du nom qui va finir" (114).

Each novel ends, then, with this melancholy idea of the extinction of the female line and the disappearance of the main character. Even the stalwart Charles had gradually begun to forget Emma:

> Une chose étrange, c'est que Bovary, tout en pensant à Emma continuellement, l'oubliait; et il se désespérait à sentir cette image lui échapper de la mémoire au milieu des efforts qu'il faisait pour la retenir. (441)

Thérèse, in the final scene of the novel, gets up from the café, where she had sat alone since Bernard's leave-taking, and "ayant gagné la rue, marcha au hasard" (115). In his preface, Mauriac can offer only the most feeble of hopes for her future well-being: "Du moins sur ce trottoir où je t'abandonne, j'ai l'espérance que tu n'es pas seule" (14).

All of these many remarkable and incontrovertible similarities between the title characters of two important modern novels, while strongly suggesting the pervasive extent of Flaubert's influence on and inspiration for the best-known of Mauriac's novels, in no way diminish the power and originality of Mauriac's fiction, whose title character remains in her own right a hauntingly enigmatic, early twentieth-century case study of "moeurs de province."[11]

In the next chapter, I attempt to sketch out psycho-sexual portraits of these two iconic heroines of modern French fiction.

NOTES

1. The expression is borrowed from the title of Harold Bloom's study *The Anxiety of Influence: a Theory of Poetry* (New York: Oxford U. P., 1975).
2. No general, comparative study of these two characters has been undertaken. There does exist, however, one article devoted to a specific theme in these two novels: Elzbieta Kowieska, "*Madame Bovary* et *Thérèse Desqueyroux*: L'Evasion impossible," *Roczniki Humanistyczne* 41, no. 5 (1993): 57-92. Jean-Hervé Donnard devotes several pages (61-66) of his *Trois Ecrivains Devant Dieu: Claudel, Mauriac, Bernanos* (Paris: Société d'Edition d'Enseignement Supérieur, 1966) to a rather diffuse comparative survey of similar elements in the two novels.
3. Kowieska, 57-58, thus summarizes the position taken by Michel Raimond in his *Le Roman contemporain: Le Signe du temps* (Paris: SEDES et CDU, 1976), 169.
4. François Mauriac, *Bloc-notes III* (1961-1964), présentation et notes de Jean Touzot, (Paris: Seuil, 1993), 172.
5. Cecil Jenkins, *Mauriac* (Edinburgh and London: Oliver and Boyd, 1965), 75.
6. Robert Speaight, *François Mauriac: A Study of the Writer and the Man* (London: Chatto and Windus, 1976), 87.
7. Anne Brunswic, C. Biet, and J.-P. Brighelli, *Flaubert: Madame Bovary* (Paris: Gallimard, 1993), 10. See also Stephen Heath, *Gustave Flaubert: Madame Bovary* (Cambridge: Cambridge U. P., 1992), 31-32, for a slightly more detailed account of the Delamare matter.
8. Jean Lacouture, *François Mauriac* (Paris: Seuil, 1980), 210. For a brief recounting of the scandalous Canaby affair dating from 1905 Bordeaux, see Lacouture, 208-210.
9. For the possible sexual implications of this and similar passages, see the second section of Chapter 2 below.
10. Dacia Maraini, *Searching for Emma: Flaubert and Madame Bovary*, tr. Vincent J. Bertolini (Chicago and London: University of Chicago Press, 1998), 71.
11. The extraordinary power Thérèse exerts on the reader has not been lost on critics who see other literary antecedents, both classical and recent, in Mauriac's heroine. Thérèse's resemblance to Phèdre, another towering example of the doomed woman, has been noted by numerous critics, among them Jean Lacouture, who sees Mauriac's title character as a Zolaesque heroine as well: "Thérèse n'est pas seulement fille de Phèdre, victime de la haine des dieux, elle est parente aussi des héroïnes 'programmées' de Zola." Lacouture refers in this latter regard to Mauriac's "plaidoyer ... pour une 'reconnaissance' de la fatalité biologique" (215).

CHAPTER II

Gender and Sexuality

Displacements of the Maternal in Flaubert's *Madame Bovary**

> "*Enfants. Affecter pour eux une tendresse lyrique, quand il y a du monde.*"
> — *Dictionnaire des idées reçues*[1]

No reader of Flaubert's *Madame Bovary: moeurs de province* can have missed the various ways in which the author suggests his eponymous heroine's social discontent with her gender. Pregnant, Emma yearns for a son and faints when her daughter is born. Anxious to be able to exercise financial control over their resources, available by law to the male head of household only, she takes the merchant Lheureux's advice and convinces Charles to grant her power of attorney; and then, with ease, manages to have him reinstate it, after Emma's mother-in-law has prevailed on Charles to revoke *la procuration*. At various times, even before, but mainly, during her affairs with Rodolphe and with Léon, Emma is seen wearing items of male attire or boldly using male accessories as part of her wardrobe.[2] Dacia Maraini, in her recent study of the novel, comments on the limited importance of these sartorial gestures:

> Once again, Flaubert brings us back to the theme of androgyny, but without ever ultimately forcing open the door to the abyss.[3]

Less apparent perhaps are the not infrequent descriptions of a Charles Bovary who exhibits feminine and, especially, maternal qualities.[4] Critical commentaries on Charles's youth usually focus on the opening pages of the novel where the narrator describes the young man's awkward first day at school and notes his limited intelligence, all the while establishing his easy good-naturedness.[5] There are clues in these early pages too, though, of a feminine side to Charles, whose ne'er-do-well father espouses an exaggerated ideal of virility:

> Sa mère le nourrissait de confitures; son père le laissait courir sans souliers, et, pour faire le philosophe, disait même qu'il pouvait bien aller tout nu, comme les enfants des bêtes. A l'encontre des tendances maternelles, il avait en tête un certain idéal viril de l'enfance, d'après lequel il tâchait de former son fils, voulant qu'on l'élevât durement, à la spartiate, pour lui faire une bonne constitution. Il l'envoyait se coucher sans feu, lui apprenait à boire de grands coups de rhum et à insulter les processions. (26)

The boy's reaction to this brutalizing, paternal regimen is clear: "Mais naturellement paisible, le petit répondait mal à ses efforts" (26). His mother's parenting efforts prove more suited to her son's temperament and, in his relationship with his own daughter, Charles will emulate his mother's behavior and eschew entirely his father's. Later in the novel, as we shall see, a similar imbalance of parental influence will be in evidence, as Charles's benevolent parenting alone has a beneficial effect on the Bovarys' daughter.

During Charles's brief first marriage, Flaubert makes clear that the masculine qualities reside not in Charles, but in the first Madame Bovary, the former *veuve* Dubuc. Describing her, Flaubert declares categorically that "sa femme fut *le maître*" (31, my emphasis). Then on the morrow, following Charles's wedding night with Emma, Flaubert strikingly uses a feminine noun to characterize the bridegroom's behavior:

> C'est lui plutôt que l'on eût pris pour *la vierge* de la veille, tandis que la mariée ne laissait rien découvrir où l'on pût deviner quelque chose. (55, my emphasis)

After the birth of their daughter Berthe, it becomes quite evident that Emma lacks even the most basic maternal qualities. It is hardly surprising that, like most women of her class (and as her own mother had done), Emma sends her infant daughter to be cared for by a wet-nurse. During her one visit to the child at *mère* Rollet's wretched hovel, accompanied by the charming Léon Dupuis, Emma assumes the most maternal of poses as she sings to the infant she has lifted into her arms. Yet this intimacy, clearly affected to impress Léon, is short-lived and such patently inauthentic gestures will be repeated but rarely. At least twice more, Emma will "perform" as loving mother for the benefit of others. (See, in this regard, the entry from Flaubert's *Dictionnaire des idées reçues* which serves as epigraph to this section). As Emma tries to suppress her passion for Léon:

> Elle retira Berthe de nourrice. Félicité l'amenait quand il venait des visites, et Mme Bovary la déshabillait afin de faire voir ses membres.

> Elle déclarait adorer les enfants; c'était sa consolation, sa joie, sa folie, et elle accompagnait ses caresses d'expansions lyriques.... (150)

Later chaffing at Rodolphe's indifference, she again "shows" her feelings for Berthe:

> —Amenez-la-moi! dit sa mère, se précipitant pour l'embrasser. Comme je t'aime, ma pauvre enfant! comme je t'aime!
> Puis, s'apercevant qu'elle avait le bout des oreilles un peu sale, elle sonna vite pour avoir de l'eau chaude et la nettoya, la changea de linge, de bas, de souliers, fit mille questions sur sa santé, comme au retour d'un voyage, et enfin, la baisant encore et pleurant un peu, elle la remit aux mains de la domestique, qui restait fort ébahie devant cet excès de tendresse. (232)

Less typical though than the several instances of theatrical, maternal concern, but more powerful in arousing the reader's animus toward the heroine, is Emma's brutal treatment of her daughter. Having returned from her fruitless encounter with the dim curate Monsieur Bournisien, a self-absorbed Emma pushes Berthe away. The child's cheek is cut and begins to bleed as she falls against a piece of furniture. At the end of this scene, Charles, the usually inept *officier de santé*, displaces Emma as the domestic care-giver and healer, while an immobilized Emma can only feign concern.

Although maternal brutality proves to be rare, indifference and disdain are not. Flaubert's puzzling silence about Emma's relationship with her own mother may well suggest, at least in part, why Emma behaves so badly toward her own daughter. If Charles learned parenting from his mother alone, Emma may well have had no such role-model in either of her parents.

In the awkward scene preceding Léon's departure from Yonville for Paris, the clerk and Emma, alone in her room, remain mute. To break the tension, Léon announces that he should like to kiss Berthe good-bye. The child is brought in; Léon kisses her several times. Then, "il la remit à sa mère," who has her taken away immediately: "Emmenez-la, dit celle-ci" (166). In almost every scene where mother and daughter are together, Emma quickly and deliberately distances herself from her child, by fainting, by violence, or by disdainful dismissal.

As a counter-weight to Flaubert's portrait of an un-motherly Emma, there emerges his portrayal of an unmistakably feminized and maternal Charles. Traditional gender categories in the novel, as in Flaubert's own life, are subverted.[6] For the most superficial of autobiographical explanations, suffice it to recall this sentence from Benjamin Bart's magistral study of the author, entitled simply *Flaubert*: "Women, Zola once said, sensed that he was a feminine type, more like them than like a man."[7]

In the face of Emma's erratic behavior and apparent ill-health following Léon's departure for Paris, Charles expresses his worry, only to have a seemingly stoic Emma dismissively make light of his concerns. This scene, highlighting the emotional distance between the spouses, is the first of many such incidents which will cause Charles to collapse into tears:

> Charles s'alla réfugier dans son cabinet; et il pleura, les deux coudes sur la table, assis dans son fauteuil de bureau, sous la tête phrénologique. (174)[8]

Similarly, after the amputation of Hippolyte's leg, following Charles's botched attempt to right the stable boy's club-foot, Emma's utter disdain for her incompetent husband again has the effect of reducing him to tears:

> Charles s'affaissa dans un fauteuil, bouleversé, cherchant ce qu'elle pouvait avoir, imaginant une maladie nerveuse, pleurant, et sentant vaguement circuler autour de lui quelque chose de funeste et d'incompréhensible. (248)

To underscore further the widening chasm which now divides the spouses, the author juxtaposes Charles's elaborate dreams of future domestic happiness with Emma's dreams of the exotic sites to which she plans to flee with Rodolphe, where "leur existence serait facile et large comme leurs vêtements de soie, toute chaude et étoilée comme les nuits douces qu'ils contemplaient" (260)—dreams to be interrupted by Berthe who "se mettait à tousser dans son berceau" (260). Charles reflects rather on his hopes for the future as he stands over Berthe's crib where, unlike Emma, he hears only his child's shallow breathing: "Il croyait entendre l'haleine légère de son enfant" (259). Somewhat earlier in the very same posture at the child's crib, Emma, as noted in Chapter 1, had had a quite different and patently unmaternal thought: "C'est une chose étrange, pensait Emma, comme cette enfant est laide!" (162). The very markers chosen to describe the child—"*son* enfant" for Charles, "*cette* enfant" for Emma—suggest their quite distinct relationships with their daughter.

Unlike Emma, Charles envisions his daughter as quite pretty:

> Ah! qu'elle serait jolie, plus tard, à quinze ans, quand, ressemblant à sa mère, elle porterait comme elle, dans l'été, de grands chapeaux de paille! on les prendrait de loin pour les deux soeurs. (259)

In stark contrast to what Flaubert calls Emma's "d'autres rêves" of flight toward self-indulgent exoticism, for Charles, in an equally idealized, but less fanciful future, it is rather his daughter who occupies the central place in this family's domesticity:

> Il se la figurait travaillant le soir auprès d'eux, sous la lumière de la lampe; elle lui broderait des pantoufles; elle s'occuperait du ménage; elle emplirait toute la maison de sa gentillesse et de sa gaieté. (259)

A poignant actualization of this projected scene will, in fact, occur later, near the end of the novel, but with modifications wholly unforeseen by Charles. For weeks, as Emma actually plans and shares the myriad details of her projected flight to Italy with Rodolphe, the question of what is to become of Berthe is never broached:

> ... et, dans tout cela, jamais il n'était question de son enfant. Rodolphe évitait d'en parler; peut-être qu'elle n'y pensait pas. (261)

Even the narratively uncertain *peut-être* does not spare Emma the ignominy of behaving here, as elsewhere, like a totally self-absorbed and utterly irresponsible mother.[9] In this way, at important moments in the novel, Flaubert tempers the reader's sympathy for a profoundly unhappy Emma by evoking disapproval as he presents her egregious failings as a mother.[10]

Flaubert describes a shift of sensibility between the spouses in the aesthetic realm too, as in the emotional and the maternal. A newly responsive Charles displaces the now disinterested Emma at the opera in Rouen. At Léon's arrival, Emma loses all interest in "Lucie de Lammermoor," Donizetti's adaptation of Sir Walter Scott's romantic tale of fatal passion, while Charles, having had, at first, some trouble following the plot, now, for the first and only time, becomes enthralled by what Emma, in a rare moment of lucidity, has just described to herself as "la petitesse des passions que l'art exagérait" (296). Charles's romantic, sentimental, and, can we say, feminine side comes to the fore as he becomes engrossed, as Emma had been until Léon appeared, in Lucia's mad scene unfolding on stage: "... restons! dit Bovary. Elle a les cheveux dénoués: cela promet d'être tragique" (300). Since Emma wants to leave, Charles, despite his new-found fascination with the performance, dutifully accedes to her wishes.

Throughout the novel, Emma proves herself to be devoid of even the most rudimentary maternal instincts in her relationship with her child. This lack does not mean, however, that she is completely un-maternal. Rather, the deficit evident in her relationship with Berthe is all the more remarkable given the surfeit of maternal concern demonstrated in her relationships with all three men with whom she is involved sexually, but especially with Léon.[11]

No fewer than three times, Emma adopts "a scornful motherly tone" with Charles.[12] Even in the early days of their marriage, Emma soon tires of Charles's constant attention and his kisses: "... elle le repoussait, à demi souriante et ennuyée, comme on fait à un enfant qui se pend après vous" (60-61). When her husband insists on smoking one of the vicomte's cigars, Emma reacts with a scold: "Tu vas te faire mal, dit-elle, dédaigneusement" (88). At the opera to quiet Charles's persistent questions about the action of the drama, her only response is an emphatic: "Tais-toi! tais-toi! fit-elle impatientée" (296). Not only to the docile Charles, but even to the stalwart Rodolphe, Emma speaks as if to a child:

> Souvent elle lui parlait des cloches du soir ou des *voix de la nature*; puis elle l'entretenait de sa mère, à elle, et de sa mère, à lui. Rodolphe l'avait perdue depuis vingt ans. Emma, néanmoins, l'en consolait avec des mièvreries de langage, *comme on eût fait à un marmot abandonné*, et même lui disait quelquefois, en regardant la lune:
> —Je suis sûre que là-haut, ensemble, elles approuvent notre amour. (229, second emphasis mine)

Just as inappropriately, Emma adopts the same maternal stance with Léon as well, but with more serious consequences:

> Elle l'appelait: "enfant."
> —Enfant, m'aimes-tu? (347)

She subsequently tightens the grip of what quickly becomes a stultifying possessiveness: "... elle lui passa autour du cou une médaille de la Vierge. Elle s'informait, comme une mère vertueuse, de ses camarades" (367-368). All this suffocating attention proves disastrous for the relationship, for Léon "se révoltait contre l'absorption, chaque jour plus grande, de sa personnalité" (367). Mario Vargas Llosa insightfully sums up the complex psychology of this skewed liaison when he writes that "precisely because Léon plays the feminine role that his energetic mistress forces upon him, Emma feels frustrated and is contemptuous of him because in her eyes he behaves like a woman...."[13]

For Charles, with Emma, as with his first wife, "sa femme fut le maître." During the last days of Emma's affair with Léon, when all her concerns are focused on the lovers' rapidly disintegrating relationship, and as Léon fitfully succumbs more and more to her motherly domination, the extent of Charles's unmasculine submissiveness and surrogate mothering becomes especially apparent. Flaubert describes the Bovary household at this period, and Charles's position in it, tellingly:

> La maison était bien triste maintenant! On en voyait sortir les fournisseurs avec des figures furieuses, il y avait des mouchoirs traînant sur les fourneaux; et la petite Berthe, au grand scandale de Mme Homais, portait des bas percés. Si Charles, timidement, hasardait une observation, elle répondait avec brutalité que ce n'était point sa faute! (373)

With Emma's attention, now more than ever, focused elsewhere, Charles fills the maternal role, first, as teacher and, then, as consoler and companion at play:

> ... il prenait la petite Berthe sur ses genoux, et, déployant son journal de médecine, essayait de lui apprendre à lire. L'enfant, qui n'étudiait jamais, ne tardait pas à ouvrir de grands yeux tristes et se mettait à pleurer. Alors il la consolait; il allait lui chercher de l'eau dans

l'arrosoir pour faire des rivières sur le sable, ou cassait les branches
de troènes pour planter des arbres dans les plates-bandes....
(373-374)

Emma is never portrayed stereotypically, telling her daughter that her busy physician-father cannot be interrupted at his work, yet Charles must remind Berthe that Emma is not to be disturbed in her self-imposed solitude:

Puis, l'enfant avait froid et demandait sa mère.
—Appelle ta bonne, disait Charles. Tu sais bien, ma petite, que
ta maman ne veut pas qu'on la dérange. (374)

Despite Emma's unabating antipathy for her daughter, on her death-bed, after an unexpected and unprecedented moment of intimacy with a desolate Charles through whose hair Emma, quite uncharacteristically, runs her fingers, the dying mother asks to see her daughter to whose naive eyes the symptoms of Emma's fatal, self-inflicted poisoning prove terrifying. Berthe's subsequent comments, echoing Little Red Riding Hood's reaction to another ravenous and devouring maternal impersonator, presage the ghastly image Emma will soon see of herself when, some moments later, she asks for a mirror:

—Oh! comme tu as de grands yeux, maman, comme tu es pâle!
comme tu sues! ...
Sa mère la regardait.
—J'ai peur, dit la petite en se reculant.
Emma prit la main pour la baiser; elle se débattait. (410)[14]

Charles, no longer able to endure this wrenching scene, has Berthe taken from the room.

Earlier, on the brink of foreclosure, Emma had imagined Charles's reaction to a putative admission of her profligacy:

... c'est moi qui t'ai ruiné, pauvre homme!
Alors ce serait un grand sanglot, puis il pleurerait abondamment,
et enfin, la surprise passée, il pardonnerait. (393)

From this moment till the end of the novel, it is the role of the weepy and forgiving spouse—accurately predicted here by Emma—and one exhibiting traditionally feminine traits, which Charles will unfailingly fill.

Following Emma's death, a more and more romantic Charles adopts Emma's ideas of fashion, such that, the narrator notes, "Elle le corrompait par-delà le tombeau" (438). Abandoned by practically everyone, Charles has but one remaining companion. Every one of his limited activities now revolves around his daughter. Ironically, the inept physician, responsible first for Hippolyte's amputated leg and then totally overcome and completely stymied at what to do during Emma's last illness, is now reduced to sewing up his daughter's dolls' stomachs: "Il racommodait ses joujoux, lui fabriquait des pantins avec des cartons, ou recousait le ventre déchiré de ses poupées" (438). At least in this childhood realm, Charles's professional competence seems not to be in doubt. And now, despite everything, he manages to realize at last the idealized, dreamed-of domestic scene of the three of them of an evening enjoying simple homey pleasures, as he manages a virtual reconstitution of the family, in spite of Emma's death, in this most melancholy scene which takes place in Emma's old room:

> ... sa chambre à elle était restée comme autrefois. Après son dîner, Charles montait là. Il poussait devant le feu la table ronde, et il approchait *son* fauteuil. Il s'asseyait en face. Une chandelle brûlait dans un des flambeaux dorés. Berthe, près de lui, enluminait des estampes. (438)

Even this most fragile and, indeed, pathetic illusion of virtual domesticity cannot last. After a final falling out between Charles and his own mother over the question of Berthe's future, the child is all that remains to him, yet this loving physician-parent is now unable to respond to his own daughter's poor health with anything save impotent alarm. All attempt at healing has been abandoned:

> A mesure que ses affections disparaissaient, il se resserrait plus étroitement à l'amour de son enfant. Elle l'inquiétait cependant; car elle toussait quelquefois, et avait des plaques rouges aux pommettes. (442)

The very final scene between father and daughter proves to be even more powerful, as the family unit, already fractured, now disintegrates entirely and irreparably. Once again, Flaubert evokes the presence of all three Bovarys in this scene. The long strand of Emma's hair, to suggest presence despite obvious absence—just as an excessively lugubrious Emma had used her own dead mother's hair to have a *tableau funèbre* fashioned—functions in much the same way as "*son* fauteuil" had in the recent bedroom gathering. The bond between Charles and his daughter, so often evident, emerges again, but this time bathed in pathos:

> A sept heures, la petite Berthe, qui ne l'avait pas vu de toute l'après-midi vint le chercher pour dîner.
> Il avait la tête renversée contre le mur, les yeux clos, la bouche ouverte, et tenait dans ses mains une longue mèche de cheveux noirs.
> —Papa, viens donc! dit-elle.
> Et croyant qu'il voulait jouer, elle le poussa doucement. Il tomba par terre. Il était mort. (445-446)

Long before Emma's death, Charles, as we have seen, had functioned as both father and as surrogate mother for their daughter. Charles's death, brought on by the irreparable pain of the loss of his faithless spouse, deprives Berthe, in the end, not only of her father, but, at the same time, of the only genuine maternal-figure she had ever known. The pathos of Charles's death and the orphaning of Berthe, followed almost immediately by the chilling news that the child has been sent to work in a cotton mill by an unnamed aunt, are juxtaposed most starkly by the author with the triumph of Homais and the well-being of his stalwart family, described as "florissante et hilaire" (442).

The asymmetry of parenting roles exhibited by the Bovarys, however understandable the causes of this imbalance might be, leads nonetheless to a desolate future for their unfortunate child. At the same time, unlike the tenderly maternal Charles, the pompous and calculating Homais, who, along with his wife, performs his parental duties in strict conformity to the accepted bourgeois pattern, is described at novel's end grandly, yet with biting irony, as "le plus heureux des pères, le plus fortuné des hommes" (442).

With the iconoclastically maternal Charles dead, the orphaned Berthe is set adrift to fend for herself as a child laborer in a mill. Earlier in the novel, Homais had expressed his enthusiasm for another such sign of industrial progress during a visit to a linen mill then under construction near Yonville. And even though Flaubert undercuts Homais' enthusiasm for the mill with the ironic comment that "Rien pourtant n'était moins curieux que cette curiosité" (144), the pharmacist's zeal for economic progress, as for traditional family values and parenting roles, clearly resonates at novel's end, as the pharmacist, not Charles, prevails. One may well appropriate Tony Williams' bleak conclusion about the broader issue of the subversion of gender stereotypes in the novel in order to characterize as well Flaubert's handling of the more precise question of paternal mothering at which Charles, despite his best efforts, eventually fails. About Flaubert's intentions, Williams concludes that: "… whilst he clearly rejects the conventional view of sexual difference, Flaubert does not offer the reader any new, heady, gender cocktail."[15] Nor any recipe for ideal parenting either.

Sexual Ambiguity in Mauriac's
Thérèse Desqueyroux

To the reader of *Thérèse Desqueyroux*, the complexity of the title character's personality and motivations is readily apparent. Critics have, in fact, suggested affinities between her and such towering fictional women as Racine's ill-fated Phèdre and, of course, to Flaubert's insatiable dreamer Emma Bovary, a resemblance chronicled in some detail in Chapter 1 above.[16]

It is for this reason then all the more surprising to encounter in an otherwise sensitive and astute critical reading of Mauriac's novel this simplistic sexual labelling of his heroine:

> So it is that Thérèse—another Lesbian—belongs not to the world of Mme. Canaby (whose physical appearance she inherits) but to the inner world of the writer himself....[17]

Simply to call Thérèse Desqueyroux a Lesbian—and with a capital L—(the capitalization is Jenkins's) is to resolve a broad and subtle network of textual ambiguities which make Mauriac's title character complex, fascinating, perplexing, and, for all these reasons, hauntingly memorable. To use the term "Lesbian" so unabashedly and unqualifiedly is to do nothing less than seriously distort the meaning of the novel and misrepresent the demonstrable intent of its author.

It is undeniable that Thérèse Desqueyroux views the activities of her marriage bed as physically repugnant. Returning to Argelouse after her acquittal, she recalls the day she married Bernard and the thoughts she had then of the approaching wedding night, the significance of which was entirely lost on her new sister-in-law Anne:

> ... la joie enfantine de la jeune fille l'isolait de Thérèse: sa joie! Comme si elle eût ignoré qu'elles allaient être séparées le soir même, et non seulement dans l'espace; à cause aussi de ce que Thérèse était au moment de souffrir.... (35)

Marriage represents for Thérèse life's watershed. As she begins her long examination of conscience, she describes her life thus:

> Tout ce qui précède mon mariage prend dans mon souvenir cet aspect de pureté; contraste, sans doute, avec cette ineffaçable salissure des noces. (25)[18]

One would be foolish to try to explain away her aversion to conjugal sex as simply a reaction to the brutish insensitivity or worse of her cloddish husband Bernard.[19] What his sexual practices were is not at all clear. That Thérèse saw what she calls "les impatientes inventions de l'ombre" (37) as abnormal and perhaps aberrant is evident, for she asks herself: "Où avait-il appris à classer tout ce qui touche à la chair—à distinguer les caresses de l'honnête homme de celles du sadique?" (36-37).

While frigid with Bernard—"je faisais la morte" (37)—Thérèse is not unreceptive to the possibility of sexual response. In fact, her conjugal submission to Bernard presages for her the possibility of other sexual feelings:

> Un fiancé se dupe aisément; mais un mari! N'importe qui sait proférer des paroles menteuses; les mensonges du corps exigent une autre science. Mimer le désir, la joie, la fatigue bienheureuse, cela n'est pas donné à tous. Thérèse sut plier son corps à ces feintes et elle y goûtait un plaisir amer. Ce monde inconnu de sensations où un homme la forçait de pénétrer, son imagination l'aidait à concevoir qu'il y aurait eu là, pour elle aussi peut-être, un bonheur possible, —mais quel bonheur? Comme devant un paysage enseveli sous la pluie, nous nous représentons ce qu'il eût été dans le soleil, ainsi Thérèse découvrait la volupté. (36)

While her sexual dislikes seem rather indisputable, her sexual preferences remain terribly imprecise. Four times in the novel, twice in the course of two different scenes, Thérèse imagines herself with a lover. The absolutely irresolvable question of the sex of her fantasy lover is striking and seems to have escaped the notice, not only of Mauriac's English translator, but also of those who have written on the novel, analyzed its heroine, and alluded to her sexuality.

The first two of these imaginings occur during successive confrontations in the garden at Saint-Clair between Thérèse and her husband's half-sister Anne de la Trave with whom Thérèse has been intimate since childhood and whose amorous liaison with Jean Azévédo she has recently decided to frustrate. Reacting to Anne's inability to describe clearly Azévédo's personality, Thérèse muses on the effect passion would have on her own powers of observation and description: "Moi, songeait Thérèse, la passion me rendrait plus lucide; rien ne m'échapperait de *l'être* dont j'aurais envie" (49, my emphasis). While there is nothing particularly unusual about Thérèse's use here of *l'être*, upon reflection, *le garçon*, which she uses several sentences earlier to refer to Azévédo, or *l'homme* might be felt in this context to be *le mot juste*. While one instance of the use of the noun *être* could be explained as a stylistic avoidance of the banal, its systematic use to the absolute exclusion of any sexually precise noun is worth noting. So it is, in a second garden conversation following hard upon the first, that Thérèse, who has begun to arouse Anne's anxiety about Azévédo's commitment to her, reflects:

> Qu'il doit être doux de répéter un nom, un prénom qui désigne *un certain être* auquel on est lié par le coeur étroitement! La seule pensée qu'il est vivant, qu'il respire, qu'il s'endort, le soir, la tête sur son bras replié, qu'il s'éveille à l'aube, que son jeune corps déplace la brume.... (51, my emphasis)

Much later during her long sequestration at Argelouse she fills her time with daydreams of other lives she might lead. She sees herself in Paris declining a young man's repeated invitations to dine, for her evenings are never free, and with reason:

> *Un être* était dans sa vie grâce auquel tout le reste du monde lui paraissait insignifiant; *quelqu'un* que personne de son cercle ne connaissait; *une créature* très humble, très obscure; mais toute l'existence de Thérèse tournait autour de ce soleil visible pour son seul regard, et dont sa chair seule connaissait la chaleur. Paris grondait comme le vent dans les pins. Ce corps contre son corps, aussi léger qu'il fût, l'empêchait de respirer; mais elle aimait mieux perdre le souffle que l'éloigner. (95-96, my emphases)

A mere five paragraphs farther on, she conjures up another scene. In this one too, her lover—now described simply with the indefinite *quelqu'un*—is again sexually undifferentiated:

> Thérèse, assise, reposait sa tête contre une épaule, se levait à l'appel de la cloche pour le repas, entrait dans la charmille noire et *quelqu'un* marchait à ses côtés qui soudain l'entourait des deux bras, l'attirait. (97-98, my emphasis)

At the very end of the novel too, it should be noted, in addition to the four key passages just cited, as Thérèse sits alone having just explained to Bernard the two irreconcilable sides of her personality, she decides not to go to see Jean Azévédo and ponders rather the chance of other encounters:

> ... elle n'avait pas envie de le voir: causer encore! chercher des formules! Elle connaissait Jean Azévédo; mais *les êtres* dont elle souhaitait l'approche, elle ne les connaissait pas; elle savait d'eux seulement qu'ils n'exigeraient guère de paroles. Thérèse ne redoutait plus la solitude. (115, my emphasis)

It is quite startling that in the standard English translation of the novel by Gerard Hopkins entitled *Therese* (New York: Farrar, Strauss and Giroux [Noonday paperback edition], 1972) the first three of these incontrovertibly ambiguous passages are systematically resolved. The ambiguous *être* is made male:

Gender and Sexuality 41

> 'Passion,' thought Thérèse, 'would make me clearer sighted. I should take note of every detail in the *man* whom I desired.' (51, my emphasis)

> How sweet it must be to say a name over and over, the pet name of the *man* to whom one's heart is tightly bound!—merely to think *he* is alive and breathing; that *he* sleeps at night with *his* head upon *his* arm, and wakes at dawn; that *his* young body plunges through the morning mist.... (53, my emphases)

> Someone was in her life who made the rest of the world seem meaningless: someone completely unknown to the rest of her circle, someone very obscure and very humble. But her whole existence revolved about this sun which she alone could see, the heat of which she only could feel upon her flesh. Paris rumbled like the sound of the wind in the pines. The sensation of her companion's body pressed against her own, light though the contact was, hindered her breathing. But rather than push *him* away she would stop breathing altogether. (109, my emphasis)

The pattern of ambiguity in the French original—albeit subtle in context—can hardly be accidental or without import. It is, in fact, highly significant and suggestive, for in the sexual realm too, as in the motivational, Thérèse, it seems clear, is incapable of absolute honesty with herself. Like her sexuality, her recollection of her role in Bernard's slow poisoning remains imprecise:

> Mais Thérèse n'a plus rien à examiner: elle s'est engouffrée dans le crime béant; elle a été aspirée par le crime; ce qui a suivi, Bernard le connaît aussi bien qu'elle-même: cette soudaine reprise de son mal .... (74)

The seemingly autonomous nature of his illness suggested by the expression "cette soudaine reprise de son mal" is echoed in the paragraphs which follow by similar descriptions of his condition. Thérèse is unwilling or, more likely, unable to own up to her active and persistent role in attempting to murder the anemic Bernard by slowly poisoning him with a prolonged series of small overdoses of an arsenic-based medicine prescribed for him to take regularly.

While Thérèse's role and responsibility in Bernard's poisoning are clearer to the reader than to her, the precise nature of her sexuality is much less clear to both character and reader. In an attempt to clarify, one could argue that the word *être*, used so consistently in her sexual fantasies, is at least once in the novel, and early on, used as a feminine substitute when Thérèse thinks in this way of the imminent loss of her virginity: "Anne demeurait sur la rive où attendaient *les êtres* intacts; Thérèse allait se confondre avec le troupeau de celles qui ont servi" (35, my emphasis); yet this single such use while suggestive of a possible feminine decoding, rather than resolving, simply underscores the sexual ambiguity of *être* when used elsewhere.[20]

Whether Thérèse Desqueyroux is a woman with deeply repressed lesbian tendencies or, given the admitted duality of her personality, a bisexual is not at all absolutely certain. What she ought certainly not to be called is simply a "Lesbian" *tout court*, as Jenkins does quite matter-of-factly in the first quote cited in this section. It is not terribly clear whether one is meant to read hers as a repressed homosexual personality, intended perhaps to complement on the internal, psychological level the constraints and limits imposed on her from without in her struggle to survive in the stifling and oppressive atmosphere of the Desqueyroux family or as bisexual. If one is to see her as the latter, is it so because she is to be construed as doomed to yearn for both kinds of love, yet to face as a consequence the impossibility of ever really knowing human love at all? She herself, of course, acknowledges her view of the divided self in her final conversation with Bernard, saying that "la Thérèse qui était fière d'épouser un Desqueyroux ... cette Thérèse-là est aussi réelle que l'autre, aussi vivante...." (112-113). Even, or especially, here though the nature of "l'autre" is undefined and unexplained.

Rather it would seem, just as Thérèse cannot explain herself, her actions or her motivations—"Etait-il vraisemblable qu'une femme de son intelligence n'arrivât pas à rendre ce drame intelligible?" (24)—that her creator does not choose entirely to do so either. Labelling Thérèse and thus narrowly defining her sexuality simplifies what is, in fact, the richly suggestive nature of her sexuality and the complexity of the total personality which Mauriac gave her and which makes her such a memorable, disturbing, and haunting character whose ambiguities resist easy resolution. To attempt to explain Thérèse Desqueyroux in terms of her sexuality alone would be an exercise as foolish and myopic as attempting, as some have, to resolve the ambiguity of her sexuality itself. While in this sexual domain Thérèse seems not at all to resemble her heterosexual antecedent Emma Bovary, the reader considering these two women together must be struck by their shared inability to achieve any sustainable sexual joy and emotional satisfaction.

NOTES

* The editors of *Romance Languages Annual* have asked for a precise notice that the first section of this chapter appeared in an earlier form as: "Displacements of the Maternal in Flaubert's *Madame Bovary*," *Romance Languages Annual*, vol. 11, 1999 (West Lafayette, IN: Purdue Research Foundation, 2000): 38-43.

1. Gustave Flaubert, *Oeuvres complètes* (Paris: Club de l'Honnête Homme, 1972), 7: 548.

2. In addition to the passage referred to in Chapter 1 describing Emma smoking and wearing a man's vest as she arrives home from Rouen, there are other references in the novel to Emma's masculine dress. Consider, for example, the following: "Elle portait, *comme un homme*, passé entre deux boutons de son corsage, un lorgnon d'écaille" (38); "... à travers son voile, qui de *son chapeau d'homme* descendait obliquement sur ses hanches, on distinguait son visage dans une transparence bleuâtre...." (215); and finally, "Elle mit *un pantalon de velours* et des bas rouges...." (377). (All the emphases here are mine).

3. Dacia Maraini, *Searching for Emma: Gustave Flaubert and Madame Bovary*, tr. V. J. Bertolini (Chicago: University of Chicago Press, 1998), 71. See also her pages 49-51. Mario Vargas Llosa, in his excellent study *The Perpetual Orgy: Flaubert and Madame Bovary*, tr. H. Lane (New York: Farrar, Straus and Giroux, 1986), 145, also comments on Emma's masculine qualities: "In Emma's case, masculinity is not only a function she must assume in order to fill a place left empty but also a striving for freedom, a way of fighting against the miseries of the feminine condition."

4. Two interesting examples of readings of traditional male religious figures as exhibiting maternal traits are found in: Caroline Walker Bynum, *Jesus as Mother: Studies in the Spirituality of the High Middle Ages* (Berkeley: University of California Press, 1982) and Rosemary Drage Hale's "Joseph as Mother: Adaptations and Appropriations in the Construction of Male Virtue," 102-116, in *Medieval Mothering*, eds. J. C. Parsons and B. Wheeler (New York: Garland, 1996).

5. For example, in a recent collection of essays on the novel, *Approaches to Teaching Flaubert's Madame Bovary*, ed. L. M. Porter and E. F. Gray (New York: MLA, 1995), while six of the nineteen essays (those by Ahearn, Bart, de la Motte, Ginsberg, McKenna, and Winchell) discuss in some detail the chapter on Emma's education, three (those by Chambers, Pinzka, and Wolf) analyze the opening pages of Part I, Chapter I, introducing Charles as he enters school to the reader.

6. Tony Williams, "Gender Stereotypes in *Madame Bovary*," *Forum for Modern Language Studies* 28, no. 2 (1992): 137, says the obvious when concluding that Flaubert, by mixing masculine and feminine traits in each of the spouses, nullifies a "hard-and-fast distinction between the sexes...." Flaubert, in fact, seems to anticipate a societal shift evident in the closing decades of the nineteenth century and described by Elaine Showalter in *Sexual Anarchy: Gender and Culture at the Fin de Siècle* (New York: Viking, 1990), 9: "What was most alarming to the *fin de siècle* was that sexuality and sex roles might no longer be contained within the neat and permanent borderlines of gender categories. Men and women were not as clearly identified and separated as they had been...."

7. Benjamin F. Bart, *Flaubert* (Syracuse: Syracuse U. P., 1967), 226.

8. Vargas Llosa, 146, writes that "In her marital relations too, the male-female roles are very soon reversed; Emma becomes the dominant personality and Charles the dominated."

9. For other examples of the lack of narrative certainty in the novel, see the first section of Chapter 5 below.

10. Michael Danahy, *The Feminization of the Novel* (Gainesville: University of Florida Press, 1991), 137, underscores even Flaubert's ambivalence toward his heroine in this way: "So Emma dared risk the consequences that would come in a society from not being the wife and mother she 'should' be, from feeling that children are not enough for an educated adult woman. The courageous side of Emma's emancipation has escaped the appreciation even of the novel's very controlled and highly self-conscious author. Thus, Flaubert saw such an attitude with the cold eye of irony or little more than silly romantic bravado in Emma. But her implicit courage did not escape the notice of another Flaubert, the artist, who was able to share his sense of this side of Emma in society."

11. In her important study *Breaking the Chain: Women, Theory, and French Realistic Fiction* (New York: Columbia U. P., 1985), 22, the late Naomi Schor, whose conclusions about Emma's maternity will be repeated later by such critics as Naomi Segal and Janet Beizer (see below), attributes this Freudian insight, *avant la lettre*, to Flaubert: "Emma will try to follow the path of integration, to accept the feminine destiny that Freud charts for the 'normal' woman: marriage and maternity. But, just as marriage ends in failure ... motherhood ends in disappointment. George, the phantom phallic-son, turns out to be only Berthe, a child worthy of Charles. Thus, much before Freud, Flaubert well understood that in order for maternity to fully satisfy penis envy, the child must be male...." Naomi Schor's remarkably insightful reading is echoed by Naomi Segal, *The Adulteress's Child: Authorship and Desire in the Nineteenth-Century Novel* (Cambridge, England: Polity Press, 1992), 122-123, and by Janet Beizer, *Ventriloquized Bodies: Narratives of Hysteria in Nineteenth-Century France* (Ithaca/London: Cornell U. P., 1994), 145-146.

12. See R. Speziale-Bagliacca, *The King and the Adulteress: A Psychoanalytic and Literary Reinterpretation of Madame Bovary and King Lear* (Durham and London: Duke U. P., 1998), 17 and 37, where he points out the second and third instances.

13. Mario Vargas Llosa, 143. In fact, all three of the men in Emma's life are weaker than she. Explaining Rodolphe's avoidance of Emma for years after the end of their affair, Flaubert writes that "il l'avait soigneusement évitée, par suite de cette lâcheté naturelle qui caractérise le sexe fort...." (400).

14. For the final exchange between the heroine and the wolf, see Charles Perrault. *Contes de ma Mère Loye*, ed. André Coeuroy (Paris: Editions de Cluny, 1948), 123. Maraini too, p. 115, notes Flaubert's use of this unmistakable intertext.

15. Williams, 138

16. See, for example, Geneviève Sutton's "Phèdre et Thérèse Desqueyroux: une communauté du destin," *FR* 43 (1970): 559-570 and Jacques Monférier's "Thérèse Desqueyroux, Phèdre et le destin," *RLM* 516-517 (1977): 109-118.

17. Cecil Jenkins *Mauriac* (Edinburgh and London: Oliver and Boyd, 1965), 74. The Mme Canaby referred to here, acquitted in 1906 by the Bordeaux Assizes of having attempted to poison her husband, was the inspiration for Mauriac's plot.

18. As noted in Chapter 1, the sexually unambivalent Emma Bovary uses almost the same expression. In reflecting at the opera on the various stages of her life, Emma thinks: "Ah! si dans la fraîcheur de sa beauté, avant *les souillures du mariage* et la désil-

lusion de l'adultère, elle avait pu placer sa vie sur quelque grand coeur solide...." (296, emphasis added).

19. Henri Peyre does as much though when he writes in *The Contemporary French Novel* (New York: Oxford U.P., 1955), 112, about Bernard that: "He is brutish and animal in his physical seizure of his bride; her senses are repelled by his complacent male coarseness." It should be said that no male character in the novel, save the nameless curate, is at all flatteringly drawn. Thérèse herself downplays any importance possibly ascribable to the young Jean Azévédo by affirming that her attempt against Bernard's life was in no way a *crime passionnel* (54).

20. It was in discussion with my former colleagues William Hendrickson and the late Richard Admussen that these mistranslations came to light. For a discussion of Mauriac's novel and the film it inspired, see R. Admussen, E. Gallagher, and L. Levin, "Novel into Film: An Experimental Course," *Literature/Film Quarterly* 6 (1978): 66-72. Naturally, critics relying on the flawed Hopkins English translation (which appeared in 1947) help perpetuate these egregious misreadings. See, for example, Michael F. Moloney, *François Mauriac: A Critical Study* (Denver: Swallow, 1958), 69ff. Another instance of the use of *être* where the word is arguable sex neutral occurs in Thérèse's poignant lament at the beginning of chapter 10:

> Me masquer, sauver la face, donner le change, cet effort que je pus accomplir moins de deux années, j'imagine que *d'autres êtres* (qui sont mes semblables) y persévèrent souvent jusqu'à la mort, sauvés par l'accoutumance peut-être, chloroformés par l'habitude, abrutis, endormis contre le sein de la famille maternelle et toute-puissante. Mais moi, mais moi, mais moi.... (87, my emphasis)

In his translation, Hopkins has arbitrarily made these beings women (!):

> Less than two years ago I might have mustered strength enough to play the hypocrite, to save my face, to put them off the scent. There are others, I suppose (*women* in all respects like me), who could go on doing that until they died; *women* who might be saved by mere habit, drugged by custom, their senses deadened; *women* who might be content to sleep in the bosom of all-powerful family. But for me—for me, for me.... (98-99, my emphases)

Note that the translation at the beginning of this English passage too is flawed and should read: "I mustered enough strength for less than two years to play...."

CHAPTER III

Religion and its Uses

The Sacraments in Flaubert's *Madame Bovary*
and
Mauriac's *Thérèse Desqueyroux*

The Christian sacraments mark the life of both individuals and of families: especially birth (Baptism), marriage (Matrimony), and death (the Anointing of the Sick, or, as it used to be called, Extreme Unction). It is of interest in considering these two novels to explore how these two very different authors have used the sacraments of the Catholic Church both to mark the important stages of the lives of the provincial French families of the title characters, and, more importantly, how scenes involving the sacraments serve to reveal aspects of these two characters' personalities.[1]

In either *Madame Bovary* or *Thérèse Desqueyroux*, and at times in both novels, there are references to Baptism, Penance, the Eucharist, Matrimony, Holy Orders (or at least its sacerdotal effects), and Extreme Unction. Only Confirmation is missing. The night of Berthe's sacramental Baptism, which is not described, Charles's father performs a mock baptism of the child using a glass of champagne, causing Bournisien to become indignant (130). As for Penance: the non-sacramental "confession" Emma attempts to make to Bournisien underscores the cleric's complete lack of sensitivity and pastoral acumen (157-158). Homais also ridicules those who send their daughters to confess to strapping men like Bournisien, for, according to the pharmacist, priests should be bled monthly in the interest of public morality (114). As for Matrimony: while the ceremony itself is not described by either Flaubert or Mauriac, in the latter's novel the stifling atmosphere of the scene in the church underscores Thérèse's predicament as she becomes part of her husband's family. She enters this family as if entering a cage (21). The reception of the sacrament of Holy Orders is not represented, but the cassock and stole, its outward signs, are referred to in both novels. Thérèse wonders what comfort the solitary curate, who exists in "the desert" created by the cassock, derives from performing his daily priestly rites (70). Homais compares Bournisien dressed in his cassock, rushing across the square to minister to the dying Emma, to crows attracted by the smell of death (415). Yet Emma finds great consolation in seeing even the dim Bournisien arrive at her sick bed. She is overcome with joy at the sight of the purple stole around his neck (415).

Upon closer scrutiny, it becomes quite apparent though that the Eucharist is the most important sacrament in both novels, for it is used by both novelists to define and reveal the personalities of the title characters. The sacrament of Extreme Unction, too, plays a major role in the celebrated, protracted deathbed scene (Part III, Chapter 8) near the conclusion of *Madame Bovary*.

Both Emma and Thérèse contemplate suicide twice, and, of course, Emma succeeds the second time. The Eucharist plays a key role in Mauriac's novel at the moment of Thérèse's failed attempt to poison herself. In Flaubert's novel too, the Eucharist figures in a scene following Emma's failed attempt at suicide prompted by her abandonment by Rodolphe on the eve of their planned flight to Italy. Emma's reception of the Eucharist, during her subsequent illness and prolonged convalescence, allows her to transcend earthly love and indulge, albeit briefly, in a sublime spiritual exaltation. Her subsequent, futile attempts to recapture this moment underscore Emma's chronic dissatisfaction with the quotidian, whether in the emotional or in the religious domain, and her quest for the unattainable sublime. In a later part of his novel, Flaubert uses the sacrament of Extreme Unction to draw to a close the highly-developed scene of Emma's death throes, as she succumbs to the fatal effects of self-inflicted, arsenic poisoning. He uses this sacrament both to recall tenderly Emma's past and to suggest the utter void which, in fact, awaits her.

Scenes involving the Eucharist are used by both novelists to highlight and to underscore the flaws of the title character. In *Madame Bovary*, Emma's reception of the viaticum, as she lies in her sick bed having been jilted by Rodolphe, sets off an emotional frenzy in which religious fervor replaces adulterous passion. Emma's dissatisfaction with life pales before the much anticipated, but disappointingly short-lived, romantically-conceived apotheosis of union with the deity. Reception of the Eucharist serves simply as a fillip which furnishes Emma the ecstatic pleasure of a brief and unrecapturable, quasi-mystical moment.

In *Thérèse Desqueyroux*, the Corpus Christi procession, during which the Eucharist is processed through the village, gives Thérèse's spouse, Bernard, that most methodical of men, the opportunity to do his duty. He alone, of all the men in the village, walks behind the priest. It is this scene, in which Thérèse execrates Bernard's hypocritical bourgeois conformism, which Thérèse will later recall as she hesitates in prayerful petition before attempting suicide.

In Flaubert's text, there is no mention of Emma on her sick bed confessing her adulterous relationship with Rodolphe before receiving the host. This preparatory step to receiving the Eucharist was perhaps omitted since she was believed to be on the verge of death. Or did Flaubert, with this lacuna, simply wish to avoid the complication of Bournisien's knowing of her adultery? In any case, she had earlier tried to talk to the priest, in a scene rich in comic misunderstandings, about her repressed passion for the then-absent Léon, only to be met by the priest's total inability to think of the suffering she referred to as anything other than physical discomfort. She was suffering, she said. He, too, found the heat oppressive, he replied (see 157).

Now, laid low by Rodolphe's abandonment of her, Emma does take communion. Anticipating receiving it:

> Sa chair allégée ne pesait plus, une autre vie commençait; il lui sembla que son être, montant vers Dieu, allait s'anéantir dans cet amour comme un encens allumé qui se dissipe en vapeur. (282)

As she receives the host: "... ce fut en défaillant d'une joie céleste," writes Flaubert. The appointments of the room and the light are transformed: "Les rideaux de son alcôve se gonflaient mollement, autour d'elle, en forme de nuées, et les rayons des deux cierges brûlant sur la commode lui parurent être des gloires éblouissantes." There follows another prolonged, grandiose celestial vision, richly described:

> ... elle laissa retomber sa tête, croyant entendre dans les espaces le chant des harpes séraphiques et apercevoir en un ciel d'azur, sur un trône d'or, au milieu des saints tenant des palmes vertes, Dieu le Père tout éclatant de majesté, et qui d'un signe faisait descendre vers la terre des anges aux ailes de flammes pour l'emporter dans leurs bras. (282)

Then as she tries to recapture these extraordinary sensations, but with less and less success, she turns—as is her custom—to material support to give life to her emotions. Just as she had earlier thought that love, like certain plants, needs a special terrain ("Ne fallait-il pas à l'amour, comme aux plantes indiennes, des terrains préparés, une température particulière?" (92)), so too now her religious ardor—this "autre amour au-dessus de tous les amours"—needs material underpinnings. Thus:

> Elle entrevit, parmi les illusions de son espoir, un état de pureté flottant au-dessus de la terre, se confondant avec le ciel, et où elle aspira d'être. Elle voulut devenir une sainte. Elle acheta des chapelets, elle porta des amulettes; elle souhaitait avoir dans sa chambre, au chevet de sa couche, un reliquaire enchâssé d'émeraudes, pour le baiser tous les soirs. (283)

Here cultic grandiosity as the source of her rapture replaces the simplicity of the Eucharistic host. Flaubert makes clear that religious ardor merely supplants carnal passion for Emma. And as she had come to tire of the latter, she will soon tire of the former:

> Quand elle se mettait à genoux sur son prie-Dieu gothique, elle adressait au Seigneur les mêmes paroles de suavité qu'elle murmurait jadis à son amant, dans les épanchements de l'adutère. C'était pour faire venir la croyance; mais aucune délectation ne descendait des cieux, et elle se relevait, les membres fatigués, avec le sentiment vague d'une immense duperie. (284)

In *Thérèse Desqueyroux*, the secularly-trained Thérèse does not undergo a Eucharist experience anything like Emma's. In fact, Thérèse avoids the curate's weekday Masses for fear of people talking of a putative conversion. Rather Bernard, her pompous, self-satisfied husband, disgusts Thérèse when he alone of the men in the village walks behind the priest who carries the Eucharist exposed in the monstrance for public adoration on Corpus Christi day. Thérèse actually has genuine religious yearnings. For Bernard, form alone is all important; the way the family is viewed by others is paramount; the preservation of its reputation justifies any means required. All must appear *comme il faut*. And so, while the rest of the men of the town simply avoid the procession for fear of having to kneel or take off their hats, Bernard processes. Thérèse recalls the scene this way:

> Bernard était presque le seul homme derrière le dais. Le village, en quelques instants, était devenu désert, comme si c'eût été un lion, et non un agneau, qu'on avait lâché dans les rues.... Les gens se terraient pour n'être pas obligés de se découvrir ou de se mettre à genoux. Une fois le péril passé, les portes se rouvraient une à une. Thérèse dévisagea le curé, qui avançait les yeux presque fermés, portant des deux mains cette chose étrange. Ses lèvres remuaient: à qui parlait-il avec cet air de douleur? Et tout de suite, derrière lui, Bernard "qui accomplissait son devoir." (72)

Later, imprisoned in the family's country house following her attempt on Bernard's life and condemned by them to what she describes as "cette agonie interminable" (88), Thérèse decides to kill herself with the very poison she had procured illegally in an attempt to kill off the boorish Bernard. Unsure, though, that death will lead to nothingness, she prays this prayer and takes a leap of faith, as hypothetical *si* gives way to the believer's *puisque* and *il* becomes a reverential *Il*:

> S'il existe cet Etre (et elle revoit, en un bref instant, la Fête-Dieu accablante, l'homme solitaire écrasé sous une chape d'or, et, cette

> chose qu'il porte des deux mains, et ces lèvres qui remuent, et cet air de douleur); puisqu'Il existe, qu'Il détourne la main criminelle avant que ce soit trop tard; —et si c'est sa volonté qu'une pauvre âme aveugle franchisse le passage, puisse-t-Il, du moins, accueillir avec amour ce monstre, sa créature. (89-90)

The sudden and quite unexpected death of Aunt Clara does, in fact, turn Thérèse's hand aside, *and* before it is too late, yet surprisingly she makes no connection between this remarkable, interruptive event and her prayer, rather: "Hasard: coïncidence. Si on lui parlait d'une volonté particulière, elle hausserait les épaules" (90).

The short-lived effect of Thérèse's act of faith and the absence of even a passing consideration of divine intervention in response to her prayer are dramatized on the Sunday following her attempted suicide and Clara's death. As she assists at Mass with Bernard and his family, her stand-off with religious faith is thrown into high relief as Mauriac compares Thérèse to a bull at the entrance to the arena:

> Un pilier la rendit invisible à l'assistance; en face d'elle, il n'y avait rien que le choeur. Cernée de toutes parts: la foule derrière, Bernard à droite, Madame de la Trave à gauche, et cela seulement lui est ouvert, comme l'arène au taureau qui sort de la nuit: cet espace vide, où, entre deux enfants, un homme déguisé est debout, chuchotant, les bras un peu écartés. (91)

The leap of faith so dramatically presented just days before—"… s'il existe … puisqu'Il existe…."—as she had contemplated taking her own life, thus has no consequence. The prayer to the divine being (*cet Être*) has been replaced, and, in its stead, the dominant image is not any longer of the Corpus Christi procession but of the Eucharistic sacrifice of the Mass, but desacralized now and seen as a bull ring before which Thérèse, like the bull, stands. Mauriac's image here is a striking one; its meaning though is less than apparent. How are we to construe it? The hostility of the scene is undeniable. The vulnerability and, indeed, the inevitable death of the animal victim, tactile. (And recall that Thérèse is often compared in the text to a tracked or a caged animal). The element of the sacred has been completely eliminated. The priest, vested on Corpus Christi day in "une chape d'or," is now described simply as "déguisé." There is no longer any reference to the Eucharist, referred to in the Corpus Christi scene as "cette chose qu'il porte," that is, the monstrance containing the consacrated Host. In spite of Thérèse's brush with belief, Mauriac will not allow the religious conversion of his murderous, yet tormented, heroine. In the preface to the novel, he tells why: "… plusieurs qui pourtant croient à la chute et au rachat de nos âmes tourmentées, eussent crié au sacrilège" (14).

The question of Flaubert's presentation of Emma's religious fate at the end of his novel is even more complex than what one finds in Mauriac's description of Thérèse following her aborted suicide attempt. Bournisien administers the sacrament of Extreme Unction to Emma as she lies on her death bed, after even the God-like Dr. Larivière has despaired of saving her life. Flaubert uses this scene of the sacrament in a number of ways: 1) through its ritual anointing of the senses, he recalls for the reader the sensual excesses of his heroine; 2) the tender and, indeed, luxurious tone and vocabulary which the author employs for this purpose underscore his empathy for his doomed eponymous heroine; 3) the end of the scene, with her short-lived turn-for-the-better and the appearance of the blind man below in the street under her bedroom window, with Emma imagining she sees his "face hideuse" as she bolts up in bed briefly before falling back lifeless, ultimately throws into question the efficacy of the sacrament. For if the sacrament of Extreme Unction has as one of its effects a "preparation for the vision of God,"[2] how then are we to react to the grotesque vision, not of hoped-for "visions de béatitude éternelle qui commençaient" (416), but of this deformed spectre? The author's intent here, as at the conclusion of his 1877 short story *Un coeur simple*, surely includes the parodic. The "face hideuse" which Emma sees and Félicité's "perroquet gigantesque" constitute parallel visions—unexpected, unnerving, and in each case utterly inappropriate, because so far removed from the orthodox beatific.[3]

The actual reception of the sacrament of Extreme Unction proceeds by stages. First comes Emma's adoration of the crucifix. The crucified Christ in this scene is described as "le corps de l'Homme-Dieu" to which she affixes "le plus grand baiser d'amour qu'elle eût jamais donné," in counterdistinction to the "baiser vorace" with which Guillaumin had just recently covered her hand in a pathetic attempt to seduce the financially ruined Emma. Flaubert's choice of the thoroughly orthodox expression "l'Homme-Dieu" to describe Christ is, of course, significant. The ancient doctrine of the hypostatic union of Christ's divine and human natures is invoked only to underscore, yet again, the fusion in Emma's mind of human sexuality and divine love. Bournisien next recites the penitential *Misereatur* and the *Indulgentiam*; and finally he anoints Emma's eyes, her nostrils, her mouth, her hands, and the soles of her feet. The prosecutor at the obscenity trial against Flaubert and his publishers said the following concerning Flaubert's description of this scene and particularly about the words of the officiating priest: "Quand on veut les reproduire, il faut le faire exactement; il ne faut pas du moins les accompagner d'une image voluptueuse sur la vie passée" (494). Yet, clearly, Flaubert did insert a whole series of voluptuous references to Emma's past as he describes the anointing of her senses:

> Le prêtre se releva pour prendre le crucifix; alors elle allongea le cou comme quelqu'un qui a soif, et, collant ses lèvres sur le corps de l'Homme-Dieu, elle y déposa de toute sa force expirante le plus grand baiser d'amour qu'elle eût jamais donné. Ensuite il récita le *Misereatur* et l'*Indulgentiam*, trempa son pouce droit dans l'huile et commença les onctions: d'abord sur les yeux, qui avaient tant convoité toutes les somptuosités terrestres; puis sur les narines, friandes

de brises tièdes et de senteurs amoureuses; puis sur la bouche, qui s'était ouverte pour le mensonge, qui avait gémi d'orgueil et crié dans la luxure; puis sur les mains, qui se délectaient aux contacts suaves, et enfin sur la plante des pieds, si rapides autrefois quand elle courait à l'assouvissance de ses désirs, et qui maintenant ne marcheraient plus. (416)

In fact, the words (or theologically speaking, the form) of the sacrament of Extreme Unction are these: "Per istam sanctam unctionem et suam piissimam misericordiam, indulgeat tibi Dominus quidquid per ... deliquisti. Amen." The formula is repeated as each faculty of the body is anointed. After the word *per* the specific faculty is named, so that anointing

the eyes, the priest says "per visum;"
the ears, "per auditum;"
the nostrils, "per odoratum;"
the mouth, "per gustum;"
the hands, "per tactum;"
and, finally, anointing the feet, "per gressum."[4]

In other words, the priest says: "Through this holy anointing and His most tender mercy the Lord pardon thee whatever sins or faults thou hast committed by sight [by hearing, smell, taste, touch, walking]."[5]

Flaubert has modified the senses anointed, inexplicably omitting the ears. He has added, though, in sonorous (note the accumulation of the sounds /s/ and /z/) and luxurious detail what precisely Emma's sins of each of the senses were:

1) les yeux, qui avaient tant convoité toutes les somptuosités terrestres;

2) les narines, friandes de brises tièdes et de senteurs amoureuses;

3) la bouche, qui s'était ouverte pour le mensonge, qui avait gémi d'orgueil et crié dans la luxure;

4) les mains, qui se délectaient aux contacts suaves;

5) et enfin sur la plante des pieds, si rapides autrefois quand elle courait à l'assouvissance de ses désirs....

According to Catholic belief, the sacrament is said to restore spiritual and, at times, physical health.[6] And Emma does seem to react positively after receiving the sacrament: "... elle n'était plus aussi pâle, et son visage avait une expression de sérénité, comme si le sacrement l'eût guérie. Le prêtre ne manqua point d'en faire l'observation" (416). And, Bournisien, as usual, makes this observation using the most hackneyed of clichés.

Like someone waking from a dream, Emma then looks around and asks for a mirror: "... et elle resta penchée dessus quelque temps, jusqu'au moment où de grosses larmes lui découlèrent des yeux. Alors elle se renversa la tête en poussant un soupir et retomba sur l'oreiller" (417). Her recovery is short-lived;

her despair at seeing herself, overwhelming; her death throes begin again almost immediately. Bournisien prays more and more rapidly as Emma's breathing becomes more and more labored. In the end, she sees not the vision of God, for which the sacrament is supposed to have prepared her, but the "face hideuse" of the blind man whose recurring presence had marked her adulterous, hebdomadal forays to Rouen.

From this examination of the role of the sacraments in *Madame Bovary* and *Thérèse Desqueyroux*, it becomes clear that two very different novelists have used commonplaces of provincial, French Catholic life more than simply to create a sense of local color or cultural authenticity. Rather, each has used the sacraments both to reveal traits of character and to suggest authorial ideology.

Mauriac almost permits Thérèse to have a religious conversion in the aftermath of the putative divine intervention which stays her self-destruction. Yet, while, as he writes in his preface to the novel, he would have liked to see her as "Sainte Locuste," the hypothetically-converted Roman poisoner, he cannot muster a justification for such a step. His self-discipline in this matter certainly saves the novel from becoming a facile moralistic tale. Thérèse's complex, and at times quite ambiguous, personality, replete with often unrealized, yet no less intense, sexual and profound religious urges, keeps the reader riveted and reflective.[7]

Flaubert, too, has used the sacraments for his own purposes. Since her days as a student at the convent of the Ursulines of Rouen, Emma had been drawn to the emotional and sentimental side of religious observance. Flaubert allows unsatisfied or waning amorous passion to be replaced in her life by intense religious sentiment, both of which though—the terrestrial and the celestial—prove to be profoundly unsatisfying. The masterfully written scene of Emma's death throes, including the reception of the sacrament of Extreme Unction, offers Flaubert, as he composed these last (w)rites, both a moment of melancholic tenderness as he recalls Emma's amorous past in loving detail and an opportunity to inject a stark reminder that death brings no consolation, no other-worldly after-life. For Emma, "la face hideuse du misérable ... se dressait dans les ténèbres éternelles comme un épouvantement" (418). If not for those present at her death, then certainly for Flaubert's readers, the chapter's last words mark an absolute and highly un-Catholic finality and one hardly consonant with the consoling aim of the sacrament of Extreme Unction: "Elle n'existait plus" (418).

Monsieur Bournisien: Flaubert's *Curé de Campagne*

The tradition of the male couple can be traced in French literature back at least to Roland and Olivier, to Marc and Tristan. And in more recent times, to cite but two examples, consider Flaubert's own Bouvard and Pécuchet, and Samuel Beckett's Estragon and Vladimir. This penultimate pair is not, however, Flaubert's only such same-sex couple. Although not title characters like the two clerks of Flaubert's final and unfinished novel, Homais, the pharmacist of Yonville, and Bournisien, the village priest, constitute another famous Flaubertian male duo. Critics have read this pair in somewhat different ways, emphasizing sometimes their similarities, sometimes their differences.

For Alison Fairlie, they form the two-panels of a nineteenth-century social diptych:

> Two pivotal figures, Homais and Bournisien are set in opposition: the lay spirit and the clerical spirit, these two vitally opposed forces in the history of nineteenth-century France, here reduced to half-baked cliché-mongers mouthing tenth-hand platitudes. Reduced intellectually, magnified comically and ironically.[8]

Dominick LaCapra sees the same obvious distinction between the two as spouters of lay and clerical commonplaces respectively, but LaCapra, in the final analysis, underscores what he sees as their remarkable similarities:

> The final scene between the priest, Bournisien, and the pharmacist, Homais, shows them in a self-parodic act of reconciliation and mutual recognition: the ultimate loving couple, they eat and sleep together over Emma's coffin. In a manner more extreme than the mingling of erotic and religious desire in Emma herself, the final embrace of these two pseudo-antagonists reveals the opposition between the sacred and the profane—like that between marriage and adultery—to be a distinction without a difference.[9]

Albert Thibaudet reads more deeply, I think, and so offers a more nuanced analysis of the two men and draws a much sharper distinction between two ostensibly similar characters who, at times, admittedly, do share traits of the buffoon. Thibaudet highlights Homais' intelligence, all the while exposing Bournisien's vapidity and utter stupidity:

> On a l'habitude de considérer Homais et Bournisien comme deux pendants, comme un bilingue de la bêtise humaine, l'un en langage religieux, l'autre en langage de la libre-pensée. Ce n'est pas exacte .... Bournisien reste au-dessous du curé moyen: c'est un magot. Au contraire, Homais dépasse le pharmacien. Intellectuel d'Yonville, il figure le Voltaire local.... Homais est intelligent. De Flaubert et de lui le plus anticlérical ce serait Flaubert, lorsqu'il fait de Bournisien la profondeur même ou l'abîme de l'imbécilité.[10]

While Thibaudet thus describes the personality and the function of each of the two antagonists, others see Bournisien as simply the unwitting *agent provocateur* of many of Homais' bombastic broadsides. And while it is indeed true, as Gérard Gengembre reminds us, that "... Bournisien vaut surtout par ce qu'il fait couple avec Homais,"[11] his subsequent agreement with Sartre's analysis of Bournisien's limited function cannot be accepted, however, without question: "Comment n'a-t-on pas vu que Bournisien est conçu tout exprès pour justifier les diatribes de Homais" (102).

Homais and Bournisien do share two major scenes (their discussion of the theatre and their vigil over Emma's corpse) and two minor ones (at the Lion d'Or before the Bovarys' arrival and in the wake of the club-foot surgery) and in each one Homais does react predictably to the presence of his feckless, clerical foil. Yet Bournisien serves other Flaubertian purposes, not the least of which, as Thibaudet so convincingly asserts, is to represent the benighted condition of the Catholic clergy in Restoration France.[12] Just as Charles, Léon, and Rodolphe serve at various times as the less than satisfying objects of Emma's amorous longings, Bournisien is the personification in the novel of religious beliefs and practices, that other significant area, along with the erotic, of Emma's yearnings and reveries.

The broad question of Flaubert's treatment of religion in *Madame Bovary* has not been the object of close and exhaustive study.[13] In an attempt to fill this gap, at least in part, I considered, in the first section of this chapter, various aspects of Catholic belief and practice and their use by Flaubert in the creation of character; viz., Emma's reception of the Eucharist and the scene, late in the novel, depicting the heroine's anointing as she receives the sacrament of Extreme Unction, the last rites of the Catholic Church. Likewise, while Homais, the pompous and opinionated pharmacist of Yonville l'Abbaye, has been the subject of a spate of studies, his nemesis and counter-weight, the curate Monsieur Bournisien, has received relatively little critical attention and when he has, critics, as we have seen, differ in their basic view of his personality and of the significance of his role in the novel.[14] In fact, the curé, that fixture of French provincial life (consider the expression: "Il pleut des curés à bicylettes") is present in the novel in roles other than Monsieur Bournisien's, although Bournisien is undeniably the embodiment, the personification, indeed the paradigm of the village priest in Flaubert's novel, subtitled, as is sometimes overlooked, "moeurs de province."

There are at least three other curates mentioned in the novel in addition to Bournsien, and they all share some aspect of his personality. Charles's nameless first teacher is described in this paragraph:

> A douze ans, sa mère obtint que l'on commençât ses études. On en chargea le curé. Mais les leçons étaient si courtes et si mal suivies, qu'elles ne pouvaient servir à grand-chose. C'était aux moments perdus qu'elles se donnaient, dans la sacristie, debout, à la hâte, entre un baptême et un enterrement; ou bien le curé envoyait chercher son élève après l'*Angélus*, quand il n'avait pas à sortir. On montait dans sa chambre, on s'installait: les moucherons et les papillons de nuit tournoyaient autour de la chandelle. Il faisait chaud, l'enfant s'endormait; et le bonhomme, s'assoupissant les mains sur son ventre, ne tardait pas à ronfler, la bouche ouverte. D'autres fois, quand M. le curé, revenant de porter le viatique à quelque malade des environs, apercevait Charles qui polissonnait dans la campagne, il l'appelait, le sermonnait un quart d'heure et profitait de l'occasion pour lui faire conjuger son verbe au pied d'un arbre. La pluie venait les interrompre, ou une connaissance qui passait. Du reste, il était toujours content de lui, disait même que *le jeune homme* avait beaucoup de mémoire. (27-28)

From these very first pages of the novel then, Flaubert presents a picture of the *curé de campagne* which is scarcely a flattering one. Lessons are tossed off in haste between a baptism and a funeral. Later, Bournisien will baptize Emma's daughter and bury the mother with about as much attention as Charles's mentor seems to have put into his own priestly duties. Charles conjugating verbs under a tree for the curate returning from taking the viaticum (the Eucharist for the sick and the dying) also resonates with Bournisien, one of whose major scenes in the novel will be as he brings the viaticum to Emma on her sick-bed, stricken after her abandonment by Rodolphe. Charles's clerical tutor does not fail to presage the future failures and the gross limitations of his soon-to-be *médecin manqué* when he summarizes the quality of his charge's efforts with a back-handed compliment: "… le *jeune homme* avait beaucoup de mémoire" (28).

The priest who teaches Charles under a tree, in the sacristy, or in his bedroom before slumbering off offers a foretaste of the distracted behavior and the intellectual shallowness of Bournisien's rote catechism lessons. The inhuman, or, at the very least, Bournisien's colossal lack of sensitivity is foreshadowed too by the repeated references to the plaster statue of a priest, described three times in the early parts of the novel. The first time is upon Emma's arrival in Tostes as Charles's new bride, where one reads that in the garden "tout au fond, sous les sapinettes, un curé de plâtre lisait son bréviaire" (58). Bournisien watching over Emma's corpse with Homais will also be depicted in the same pose and, like Charles's teacher, he too will doze off and begin to snore: "Monsieur Bournisien, plus robuste [que Homais], continua quelque temps à remuer tout bas les lèvres, puis insensiblement, il baissa le menton, lâcha son gros livre noir et se mit à ronfler" (426).

The priestly statue reappears twice more before the Bovarys' arrival at Yonville. During the depressing days of her first winter with Charles, Emma goes into the garden on those rare sunlit days and it is there where "on n'entendait pas d'oiseaux," where "tout semblait dormir," and where she sees not only "la vigne comme un grand serpent malade," but also this: "Dans les sapinettes, près de la haie, le curé en tricorne qui lisait son bréviaire avait perdu le pied droit, et même le plâtre, s'écaillant à la gelée, avait fait des gales blanches sur sa figure" (97).

The statue now falling apart bears the same kind of disfigurement to be worked on Hippolyte, whose leg will be amputated as a result of Charles's ineptitude, while its facial blemishes are shared not only by Homais, whose face has been left scarred by small pox, but by the blind beggar, who will appear as the unseeing witness to Emma's adultery and whose "face hideuse" will come to represent for Emma, not the consolations of the afterlife, but, rather, what horror she feels awaits her in the beyond.

The themes of degeneration and annihilation are found throughout the novel and the priest's statue, making its final appearance, constitutes a link in this thematic network as the Bovarys move from Tostes to Yonville l'Abbaye. Flaubert explains the name of their new town thus: "... ainsi nommé à cause d'une ancienne abbaye de Capucins, dont les ruines n'existent même plus" (105). While the abbey has left no trace, the village church does still stand, rebuilt entirely during the last years of the reign of Charles X (reign: 1824-1830) and yet, despite the recent construction: "La voûte en bois commence à se pourrir par le haut, et de place en place, a des enfonçures noires dans sa couleur bleue" (107).

It is soon after arriving in a decaying Yonville that Charles's disquietude is explained by the lack of patients, by money worries, and by the damage done to their belongings during the move: "... que de choses endommagées ou perdues dans le transport de Totes à Yonville, sans compter le curé de plâtre, qui, tombant de la charrette à un cahot trop fort, s'était écrasé en mille morceaux sur le pavé de Quincampoix" (127).

At Yonville, the void left by the disappearance of the Capuchins and by the destruction of the plaster priest will be filled by Monsieur Bournisien, whose introduction into the story Flaubert had effected several pages earlier on, as the author quickly passed in review all the major inhabitants of the town. Flaubert describes this character physically even before making his identity clear:

> ... Madame Lefrançois alla sur le seuil regarder si l'*Hirondelle* n'arrivait pas. Elle tressaillit. Un homme vêtu de noir entra tout à coup dans la cuisine. On distinguait, aux dernières lueurs du crépuscule, qu'il avait la figure rubiconde et le corps athlétique.
> —Qu'y a-t-il pour votre service, monsieur le curé? demanda la maîtresse d'auberge.... (113)[15]

Offered a drink, he refuses; he asks that his umbrella, forgotten at the convent at Eremont, be delivered to the rectory; and he leaves "pour se rendre à l'église, où l'on sonnait l'Angélus" (114). His first encounter with Emma, too, during which he will fail totally to grasp the cause and nature of her anguish will take place at the church to which this same Angelus bell will have drawn Emma.

This brief appearance of the curate at the Lion d'Or precipitates Homais' first overblown, anticlerical outburst, including a totally gratuitous attack on tithing:

> Ce refus d'accepter un rafraîchissement lui semblait une hypocrisie des plus odieuses; les prêtres godaillaient tous sans qu'on les vît, et cherchaient à ramener le temps de la dîme. (114)

Madame Lefrançois defends Bournisien, citing his recent help with the crops when he carried six bales at a time, adding "tant il est fort." She thus furnishes the chemist with another subject for his spleen:

> —Bravo! dit le pharmacien. Envoyez donc vos filles en confesse à des gaillards d'un tempérament pareil! Moi, si j'étais le gouvernement, je voudrais qu'on saignât les prêtres une fois par mois. Oui, madame Lefrançois, tous les mois, une large phébotomie, dans l'intérêt de la police et des moeurs! (114)

At Bournisien's next appearance, he is paired, not with Homais, but with Charles's father, for both the curate and Berthe's paternal grandfather will baptize the child. Bournisien's orthodox ceremony is not described in the novel, but referred to simply in the introductory sentence to a scene which takes place later that same day: "Le soir de la cérémonie, il y eut un grand dîner; le curé s'y trouvait; on s'échauffa" (130). After songs by Homais, Léon, and Madame Bovary *mère*, Charles's father takes center stage:

> ... enfin M. Bovary père exigea que l'on descendît l'enfant, et se mit à le baptiser avec un verre de champagne qu'il lui versait de haut sur la tête. Cette dérision du premier des sacrements indigna l'abbé Bournisien; le père Bovary répondit par une citation de *la Guerre des dieux*, le curé voulait partir; les dames suppliaient; Homais s'interposa; et l'on parvint à faire rasseoir l'ecclésiastique, qui reprit tranquillement, dans sa soucoupe, sa demi-tasse de café à moitié bue. (130)

Again the curate behaves in a perfectly correct way in the face of the elder Monsieur Bovary's anticlericalism which is at times even more pronounced than Homais'. Not only had his father tried to get the mild-mannered Charles as a boy to make fun of religious processions (26), but he himself annually scandalized his long-suffering wife by ordering each Good Friday, the most solemn day of abstinence in the liturgical year, pork sausage (285).

Just as Homais had suggested that the robust and virile Bournisien ought to be bled because of the threat he posed to the virtue of his young female parishioners, Madame Bovary *mère* presses for an early departure from Yonville because she fears her husband may exert an immoral influence on the thinking of Charles's young wife, whom the father-in-law sometimes grabs round the waist, while warning Charles "prends garde à toi" (131). The narrator then adds tentatively that Charles's mother might have even more serious concerns: "Peut-être avait-elle des inquiétudes plus sérieuses. M. Bovary était un homme à ne rien respecter" (131).[16]

And so if there are licentious priests, as Homais contends, there is no indication at all that Bournisien is to be counted among them. In this domain, at least, he might best be described by the second half of the entry in the *Dictionnaire des idées reçues* on "Prêtres:" "Couchent avec leurs bonnes et ont des enfants qu'ils appellent leurs neveux. —C'est égal, il y en a de bons, tout de même!"[17]

While apparently faithfully celibate, Bournisien's priestly talents are found to be terribly wanting in his next scene with the title character. Emma's repressed passion for Léon weighs so heavily on her that one April evening, while looking out her window, the repeated ringing of the Angelus awakens old memories of the religious fervor of her convent days:

> Alors un attendrissement la saisit; elle se sentit molle et tout abandonnée, comme un duvet d'oiseau qui tournoie dans la tempête; et ce fut sans en avoir conscience qu'elle s'achemina vers l'église, disposée à n'importe quelle dévotion, pourvu qu'elle y absorbât son âme et que l'existence entière y disparût. (156)

Her romantic longings for an end to her anguish will now be dashed repeatedly during a conversation with a Bournisien totally incapable of understanding the language of the emotions. For him, all is practical and literal, as is clear from their very initial exchange:

> —Comment vous portez-vous? ajouta-t-il.
> —Mal, répondit Emma; je souffre.
> —Eh bien! moi aussi, reprit l'ecclésiastique. Ces premières chaleurs, n'est-ce pas! vous amollissent étonnamment. Enfin, que voulez-vous? nous sommes nés pour souffrir, comme dit saint Paul. (157-158)

Emma tries to tell him that Charles cannot help her, for "ce ne sont pas les remèdes de la terre qu'il me faudrait" (158). He barely hears her, distracted as he is by the unruly children he is preparing for first communion and his need to tell her an inane *jeu de mots* with which he had been able to elicit a laugh from the bishop. Emma persists, fixing "sur le prêtre des yeux suppléants" and saying: "Oui ... vous soulagez toutes les misères" (158). Again, Bournisien can understand only physical suffering and tells her the story of peasants who had recently called him to their farm because their cow, whom they thought possessed, had gas.[18]

In desperation, Emma tries a third time. When Bournisien says that the farmers are to be pitied, Emma retorts: "Il y en a d'autres" (159). The curate agrees, citing workers in towns; homemakers, models of virtue, but starved for want of bread, or lacking a fire in winter. Before this absolutely impenetrable wall of insensitivity, Emma finally surrenders in utter despair: "Eh! qu'importe" (159).

This scene, powerfully effective in arousing our sympathy for a troubled Emma, reveals to the reader for the first time Bournisien's profound and utter pastoral ineptitude. Flaubert, in his correspondence, had this to say about this scene and his clerical creation:

> ... elle [Emma] trouve à la porte le curé qui, dans un dialogue (sans sujet déterminé), se montre tellement bête, plat, inepte, crasseux, qu'elle s'en retourne dégoûtée et indévote. Et mon curé est très brave homme, excellent même, mais il ne songe qu'au physique (aux souffrances des pauvres, manque de pain ou de bois), et ne devine pas les défaillances morales, les vagues aspirations mystiques; il est très chaste et pratique tous ses devoirs.[19]

The famous Comices Agricoles episode (I, 8) offers the reader the third (along with Charles's mentor and the plaster priest) of the trio of other curates in a long chapter which ends with a reference to Bournisien's absence from this central part of the novel. Just as Félicité in *Un coeur simple* (1877) will offer Loulou, her stuffed parrot, to her village priest to decorate the temporary altar erected below her window for the Corpus Christi celebration, so too in *Madame Bovary* another example of "un demi-siècle de servitude," Catherine Leroux, will offer her "médaille d'argent—du prix de vingt-cinq francs" (205) to her parish priest who in exchange will say Masses which, one assumes, will be Masses for the repose of her soul to be celebrated after her death: "Je la donnerai au curé de chez moi, pour qu'il me dise des messes" (205). The pathos of this faithful servant so powerfully evoked by the author, who describes her qualities thus: "Dans la fréquentation des animaux, elle avait pris leur mutisme et leur placidité" (204), is undercut by Homais who has the final word on the matter: "Quel fanatisme! exclama le pharmacien, en se penchant vers le notaire" (205).

Homais' journalistic reportage about the fair, in which he transforms the events with fabulous embellishments and outright lies, ends with another attack on the clergy, and, this time, Bournisien himself is the target; yet a Bournisien curiously elevated from potential deflowerer of village virgins to wily Jesuit:

> On y a seulement remarqué l'absence du clergé. Sans doute les sacristies entendent le progrès d'une autre manière. Libre à vous, messieurs de Loyola! (209)[20]

Here, from the *Dictionnaire des idées reçues*, is Flaubert's description of "Jésuites:" "Ont la main dans toutes les révolutions. —On ne se doute pas du nombre qu'il y en a...." (310). Surely, the dim Bournisien cannot be among their number, no matter how great it might be!

Although not present at the Comices Agricoles, Bournisien is not at all absent from the club-foot episode, where he attempts again to exercise his pastoral vocation in counseling the hapless victim of Charles and Homais, or as Flaubert sardonically refers to them "les deux savants" (240), who, having opened the post-surgical contraption holding in place Hippolyte's gangrenous foot, observe the putrefaction of the limb and rebuckle it in the box even more tightly "pour accélérer les choses" (240).

Speaking with Hippolyte, Bournisien uses the same inappropriate logic he will later use with Charles after Emma's death, urging, not just acceptance, but joy and thanks for suffering. First, with the stable boy:

> Il commença par le plaindre de son mal, *tout en déclarant qu'il fallait s'en réjouir*, puisque c'était la volonté du Seigneur, et profiter vite de l'occasion pour se réconcilier avec le ciel. (241, my emphasis)

And with Charles:

> Il [Bournisien] discourait sur la vanité des choses terrestres. Dieu était bien grand, bien bon; on devait sans murmure se soumettre à ses décrets, *même le remercier.* (421, my emphasis)

Bournisien admonishes Hippolyte for his dereliction of his religious duties and concludes: "Mais à présent, c'est l'heure d'y réfléchir" (242). Then, using clichés rife with hyperbole, he continues, realizing himself, by the inflection apparent in the parenthetical, that the hackneyed phrase "about to meet their maker" is hardly comforting even as he utters it. "Ne désespère pas cependant, j'ai connu de grands coupables qui, près de comparaître devant Dieu (tu n'en es point encore là, je le sais bien) avaient imploré sa miséricorde, et qui certainement sont morts dans les meilleures des positions" (242).

He then asks Hippolyte to pray morning and night adding: "Oui, fais cela! pour moi, pour m'obliger. Qu'est-ce que ça coûte?...." (242). Bournisien's sophistic strategy will be used again in the novel, when Maître Dubocage, at the request of Léon's mother, warns his clerk of the dangers of a liaison with "une femme mariée" and asks him to break it off: "Il le supplia de rompre, et, s'il ne faisait ce sacrifice dans son propre intérêt, qu'il le fît au moins pour lui, Dubocage!" (375).

Bournisien's visits and admonitions succeed so well that Hippolyte, having agreed to pray as asked, now proposes to make a pilgrimage if he is cured.[21] Bournisien, going Pascal one better so that two *paris* are better than one, assures him that an extra precaution can only help: "... à quoi M. Bournisien répondit qu'il ne voyait pas d'inconvénient; deux précautions valaient mieux qu'une. *On ne risquait rien*" (242). To this clerical odds-making, there is a double reaction. Not unexpectedly, "L'apothicaire s'indigna contre ce qu'il appelait les *manoeuvres* du prêtre; elles nuisaient, prétendait-il, à la convalescence d'Hippolyte...." (242). The narrator's subsequent reaction also ridicules too the efficacy of Bournisien's pair of precautions and of the Charles-Homais medical adventurism as well: "Cependant la religion pas plus que la chirurgie ne paraissait le secourir, et l'invincible pourriture allait montant toujours des extrémités vers le ventre" (243). Bad medicine and superstitious religious bargaining are both dismissed as worthless. LaCapra's suggested leveling of Homais and Bournisien could well be applied to this scene, as well as to his reading of their behavior during Emma's wake.

While Hippolyte's prayers and pious promises are familiar territory for Bournisien, the mystical *élans* of Emma's recuperation are well beyond the curate's limited experience, so that he is both impressed and, at the same time, disturbed by them: "Le curé s'émerveillait de ces dispositions, bien que la religion d'Emma, trouvait-il, pût, à force de ferveur, finir par friser l'hérésie et même l'extravagance" (283). The latter transgression seems to him more serious than the former! Unsure, therefore, of how to proceed, Bournisien writes to the bishop's bookseller for "*quelque chose de fameux pour une personne du sexe, qui était pleine d'esprit*" (283). Bournisien's oral platitudes will be reinforced now by published ones. Even though Emma will be put off by the hodge-podge sent by the bookseller "avec autant d'indifférence que s'il eût expédié de la quincaillerie à des nègres," yet, when fatigued, the book falling from her hand, Emma "se croyait prise par la plus fine mélancolie catholique qu'une âme éthérée pût concevoir" (284). But like Hippolyte's devotions, Emma's too will be short-lived and ineffectual. As she recovers, all her fervor will be replaced by indifference and, in the end, she even "fréquenta l'église avec moins d'assiduité ...." (286). Thus Bournisien's loss is perceived by Homais as his gain because her cooling to religious practice was "à la grande approbation de l'apothicaire, qui lui dit alors amicalement: —Vous donniez un peu dans la calotte!" (286). With "un peu," even Homais is capable of understatement.

While Emma strays from her devotions, Bournisien does not abandon the Bovarys and it is during one of his afternoon visits that he and Homais, in the company of Charles and Binet, engage in the first of their two major scenes together, during which each will espouse his views on, of all subjects, the theatre. Bournsien's utter lack of originality is made manifest at the very start of the discussion. Binet, as is the custom, uncorks the bottle "... le cidre, pendant sa démonstration, souvent leur jaillissait en plein visage, et alors l'ecclésiastique, avec un rire opaque, ne manquait jamais cette plaisanterie: —Sa bonté saute aux yeux!" (287).

The theatre discussion begins when Homais' proposal that Charles take Emma to hear the tenor Lagardy at the opera house in Rouen as part of her convalescence, to the pharmacist's amazement, does not scandalize the cleric. Bournisien, the reader learns, considers "la musique comme moins dangereuse pour les moeurs que la littérature" (287). (One can imagine Flaubert's sly smile at the writing of this line). Bournisien admits there are good plays and good playwrights; it is rather the seductive charms of theatrical productions which disturb him:

> ... cependant, ne serait-ce que ces personnes de sexe différent réunies dans un appartement enchanteur, orné de pompes mondaines, et puis ces déguisements païens, ce fard, ces flambeaux, ces voix efféminées .... (288)

And so he concludes that "tout cela doit finir par engendrer un certain libertinage d'esprit et vous donner des pensées déshonnêtes, des tentations impures" (288). While Bournisien's description seems absurdly exaggerated and the dangers he evokes vastly overstated, in the very next chapter Emma, during the production of *Lucie de Lammermoor*, will have just such "pensées déshonnêtes" and "des tentations impures" as she becomes enamored, first, of Lagardy and, then, in a furor of sexual excitement, again meets Léon, now ready for much more than a platonic relationship with the eponymous heroine. But, it certainly must be remembered that Emma is hardly your average theatre-goer.

Bournisien's concern for the dangers inherent in worldly pleasures and his blind adherence to the discipline of the Church are now expressed in another Flaubertian master phrase, but one where the cleric's own indulgence in a pinch of snuff undercuts both his ideas and his unusually lofty tone:

> Enfin, ajouta-t-il en prenant subitement un ton de voix mystique, tandis qu'il roulait sur son pouce une prise de tabac, si l'Eglise a condamné les spectacles, c'est qu'elle avait raison; il faut nous soumettre à ses décrets. (288)

Just as he had admonished Hippolyte, and as he will soon admonish Charles, to submit without murmuring to the will of God, here also, for the curate, the appeal to Church authority settles the matter. One almost expects him to resort to Latin, as Homais sometimes does, and declare "Roma locuta est, causa finita est." Homais warms to the debate as he expounds on his own mangled version of medieval theatre history: why would the Church object to the theatre when it had allowed in the very naves of its churches "des espèces de farces appelées mystères, dans lesquelles les lois de la décence souvent se trouvaient offensées" (288).

It is a short leap for Homais from the bawdiness of medieval religious theatre to the Bible and he can hardly contain himself as he soldiers on, blusteringly: " —C'est comme dans la Bible; il y a ... , savez-vous ... , plus d'un détail ... piquant, des choses ... vraiment ... gaillardes!" (288). Homais is certain the Bible is not a book to be put into the hands of the young, to which Bournisien offers with marvelous obfuscation this delicious retort: "Mais ce sont les protestants, et non pas nous, s'écria l'autre impatienté, qui recommandent la Bible!" (288).

Homais continues in order to antagonize Bournisien further: "J'en ai connu, des prêtres, qui s'habillaient en bourgeois pour aller voir gigoter des danseuses" (289). Bournisien demurs; Homais insists: "J'en-ai-con-nu" (289). To which testimony, the cleric can only agree: "Eh bien, ils avaient tort, dit Bournisien résigné à tout entendre" (289). In the face of such docility, Homais cannot not add: "—Parbleu, ils en font bien d'autres!" (289). At that, Bournisien, no longer able to use restraint or retort, uses anger in response, as he will later and as he had at Berthe's mock-baptism: "Monsieur! ... reprit l'ecclésiastique avec des yeux si farouches, que le pharmacien en fut intimidé" (289).[22]

In the face of Bournisien's rage, the unheroic Homais can only desist and offer a lame excuse:

>—Je veux seulement dire, repliqua-t-il alors d'un ton moins brutal, que la tolérance est le plus sûr moyen d'attirer les âmes vers la religion. (289)

Cowed into being agreeable in Bournisien's presence, Homais claims victory and regains his boldness following the priest's departure, suggesting Charles should, like him, enjoy inciting the priest's rage:

>—Voilà ce qui s'appelle une prise de bec! Je l'ai roulé, vous avez vu, d'une manière!... Enfin, croyez-moi, conduisez Madame au spectacle, ne serait-ce que pour faire une fois dans votre vie enrager un de ces corbeaux-là, saprelotte! (289)

During Emma's subsequent hebdomadal, adulterous excursions to Rouen, Bournisien, like Homais and Lheureux, serves as a witness of sorts to her infidelity. One Thursday, Charles gives the priest her shawl, asking him to deliver it to her at the Croix Rouge in Rouen. When the proprietor tells him that the wife of the doctor from Yonville rarely frequents his inn, Bournisien makes nothing of this remark:

>Aussi, le soir, en reconnaissant Madame Bovary dans l'*Hirondelle*, le curé lui conta son embarras, sans paraître, du reste, y attacher de l'importance; car il entama l'éloge d'un prédicateur qui pour lors faisait merveille à la cathédrale, et que toutes les dames couraient entendre. (353)

All women, that is, except Emma whose activities at the cathedral and in Rouen are of an different sort entirely.

During Emma's convalescence, Flaubert had used synecdoche to describe the calming effect, not so much of Bournisien personally, but of a sacerdotal presence:

> C'était à cette heure-là que M. Bournisien venait la voir. Il s'enquérait de sa santé, lui apportait des nouvelles et l'exhortait à la religion dans un petit bavardage câlin qui ne manquait pas d'agrément. La vue seule de sa soutane la réconfortait. (281)

Now, during her death throes after swallowing handfuls of arsenic, Emma again finds solace, not so much in Bournisien's arrival, but at the sight of the symbol of his priestly authority. She does not now notice his cassock, while Homais does and with an unpleasant reaction, "car la soutane le faisait rêver au linceul, et il exécrait l'une un peu par l'épouvante de l'autre" (415). Emma fixes her attention on something else:

> Elle tourna sa figure lentement, et parut saisie de joie à voir tout à coup l'étole violette, sans doute retrouvant au milieu d'un apaisement extraordinaire la volupté perdue de ses premiers élancements mystiques, avec des visions de béatitude éternelle qui commençaient. (415-416)

After anointing her, Bournisien attempts to place a lighted candle in her hand as a symbol of her imminent celestial glory. Without his help, she cannot hold on to it. Despite this disturbing sign, Bournisien proceeds to suggest a turn for the better:

> Cependant elle n'était plus aussi pâle, et son visage avait une expression de sérénité, comme si le sacrement l'eût guérie.
> Le prêtre ne manqua point d'en faire l'observation; il expliqua à Bovary que le Seigneur, quelquefois, prolongeait l'existence des personnes lorsqu'il le jugeait convenable pour leur salut; et Charles se rappela un jour où, ainsi près de mourir, elle avait reçu la communion.
> —Il ne fallait peut-être pas se désespérer, pensa-t-il. (416-417)

While Charles's optimism is misplaced, as is Bournisien's, it is the latter kneeling in his flowing cassock, nonetheless, who occupies the central place in this death scene:

> Bournisien s'était remis en prière, la figure inclinée contre le bord de la couche, avec sa longue soutane noire qui traînait derrière lui dans l'appartement. (417)

It is the priest who fills the room too with his voice, whose effect is quite extraordinary:

> A mesure que le râle devenait plus fort, l'ecclésiastique précipitait ses oraisons; elles se mêlaient aux sanglots étouffés de Bovary, et quelquefois tout semblait disparaître dans le sourd murmure des syllabes latines, qui tintaient comme un glas de cloche. (417)

Bournisien's presence and voice will thus dominate the scene of the heroine's death, but only until the arrival of the blind man whose voice and image will displace Bournisien's, whose bawdy song will drown out the cleric's prayers, and whose face for Emma "se dressait dans les ténèbres éternels comme un épouvantement" (418). Neither the penitential purple stole, the black cassock, not Bournisien's anointing, nor his prayers, nor the lighted candle he places in her hand seem able to console Emma at her end. Again, as in the case of the club-footed Hippolyte, religion no more than medicine is of any help.

The second and final major confrontation between Bournisien and Homais will take place as they watch together over the heroine's corpse the night before her burial. All the while they will ignore her presence and grudgingly suffer several interruptions as Charles returns again and again, drawn inexorably to Emma. The cleric and the pharmacist again take up their usual debating stances: the curate defending religious practice, the rationalist attempting its disparagement. Bournisien defends the ancient Catholic belief in the efficacy of prayers for the dead; but for Homais, these are useless, for either Emma died in the state of grace and, therefore, needs no prayers or she died unrepentant and prayers can in no way now effect her salvation (422). The pharmacist then lets loose a double volley of clichés. Homais admires Christianity, he says, for freeing the serfs and for giving the world a morality, but as for the authority of sacred text, they were all fabricated by the Jesuits.

For none of this does Bournisien have any answer. He doesn't use anger as a reaction, as he does elsewhere, but simply either *ad hominem* arguments or appeals to authority. To counter Homais' attack on prayer, Bournisien retorts: "—Comment! ... la prière! Vous n'êtes donc pas chrétien?" (422). To show there is more to Christianity than freedom for the serfs, Bournisien can only reject Homais' arguments out of hand and invoke the authority of Scripture: "—Il ne s'agit pas de cela! Tous les textes...." (422). Homais in turn rejects the authenticity of the texts, for "... on sait qu'ils ont été falsifiés par les Jésuites" (422).

They take up their discussion again, after Charles who had come upstairs leaves, tossing off partisan book titles like so many ineffectual, verbal grenades. Anger now overcomes them both: "... Bournisien se scandalisait d'une telle audace; Homais s'émerveillait d'une telle bêtise; et ils n'étaient pas loin de s'adresser des injures" (423), when Charles again interrupts them.

Charles's inconsolable grief now furnishes them with yet another topic. Homais congratulates Bournisien for not being subject, like everyone else, to losing a spouse. Bournisien can defend clerical celibacy only ever so feebly, citing the danger a spouse would represent for the sanctity of the seal of the confessional: "... voulez-vous qu'un individu pris dans le mariage puisse garder, par exemple, le secret de la confession?" (425). Hardly a satisfying answer for Homais and so: "Homais attaqua la confession" (425). The practical Bournisien can think only of utilitarian benefits, not spiritual ones, offered by the sacrament of Penance: "... il s'étendit sur la restitution qu'elle faisait opérer. Il cita différentes anecdotes de voleurs devenus honnêtes hommes tout à coup." And then he gives this curious example: "Des militaires ... avaient senti les écailles leur tomber des yeux" (425-426).

To all this, Homais offers no response, for he has fallen asleep during Bournisien's disquisition on the practical benefits of the sacrament of Penance. Awakened by the priest, Homais comments on a barking dog in the distance. At the mention of this sound, Bournisien finds himself on more familiar ground than theology or Church history and so enumerates popular superstitions on the reactions of animals to human deaths:

> On prétend qu'ils [les chiens] sentent les morts.... C'est comme les abeilles: elles s'envolent de la ruche au décès des personnes. (426)

The two men then sleep and Flaubert describes them rather tenderly as "... après tant de désaccord se rencontrant enfin dans la même faiblesse humaine; et ils ne bougeaient pas plus que le cadavre à côté d'eux qui avait l'air de dormir" (426).

At the end of this long night, after each one of them has aspergé the room—Bournisien with holy water, Homais with chorine water—, they share the brandy, brioche, and camembert left for them by Félicité, eating only after Bournisien has gone out to say Mass so that, upon returning to the Bovarys', he can break his Eucharistic fast: "... puis ils mangèrent et trinquèrent, tout en ricanant un peu, sans savoir pourquoi, excités par cette gaieté vague qui vous prend après des séances de tristesse" (428). It is Bournisien who then concludes the scene in a spirit of bonhomie: "... et au dernier petit verre, le prêtre dit au pharmacien, tout en lui frappant sur l'épaule: —Nous finirons par nous entendre!" (428). Emma through this long night has been almost totally eclipsed by this Yonvillian version of the vaudevillian cross-talk of a proto-typical Estragon and Vladimir.

Bournisien will again overshadow Emma at her own funeral Mass:

> M. Bournisien, en grand appareil, chantait d'une voix aiguë; il saluait le tabernacle, élevait les mains, étendait les bras....
> On chantait, on s'agenouillait, on se relevait, cela n'en finissait pas! (431)

Just as earlier in response to Bournisien's demand for gratitude to God for having taken Emma to which Charles had responded: "Je l'exècre votre Dieu" (421), now in the face of all these seemingly endless, pious actions Charles reacts similarly:

> Mais quand il pensait qu'elle se trouvait là-dessous, et que tout était fini, qu'on l'emportait dans la terre, il se prenait d'une rage farouche, noire, désespérée. (431)

Bournisien's final act in the novel will similarly evoke for Charles, and the reader, both the finality of death and the priest's pairing with the pharmacist:

> Alors Bournisien pris la bêche que lui tendait Lestiboudois; de sa main gauche, tout en aspergeant de la droite, il poussa vigoureusement une large pelletée; et le bois du cercueil, heurté par les cailloux, fit ce bruit formidable qui nous semble être le retentissement de l'éternité.
> L'ecclésiastique passa le goupillon à son voisin. C'était M. Homais. (433)

Bournisien's role in the novel does not end here in the graveyard at Emma's tomb. One short paragraph in the final chapter of the novel describes both his subsequent pastoral activities and the upshot of his suggestion that he and Homais—whom Thibaudet calls, as we have seen, *le Voltaire local*—will end up getting along:

> On le [Charles] vit pendant la semaine entrer le soir à l'église. M. Bournisien lui fit même deux ou trois visites, puis l'abandonna. D'ailleurs, le bonhomme tournait à l'intolérance, au fanatisme, disait Homais; il fulminait contre l'esprit du siècle, et ne manquait pas, tous les quinze jours, au sermon, de raconter l'agonie de Voltaire, lequel mourut en dévorant ses excréments, comme chacun sait. (441-442)

What becomes of most of the other characters, Flaubert tells with a certain finality as the novel comes to an end. Léon marries Léocadie Leboeuf; Justin leaves Yonville for Rouen; Charles drops dead, as does his mother; Berthe is sent to a cotton mill; and, of course, Homais is awarded the Croix d'Honneur. There is no particular dénouement, however, for Bournisien. This *curé de campagne* will go on offering his meager brand of spiritual comfort, blustering against Voltairian free-thinkers, and continuing to personify for Flaubert's readers "la profondeur ou l'abîme de l'imbécilité."[23]

The second section on "Alterity in *Thérèse Desqueyroux*" in Chapter 5 below treats Mauriac's country priest who plays a less pervasive role than Bournisien, yet an important one as the heroine's imagined exemplar and, at the same time, as yet another object of the family's harsh criticism and condemnation of those different from themselves.

NOTES

1. While Mauriac's Catholicism distinguishes him sharply in belief from the hermit of Croisset, the affinity between the two men is more telling than the obvious similarities between the two fictional women they created. Let's recall that Cecil Jenkins, *Mauriac* (Edinburgh and London: Oliver and Boyd, 1965), 75, quotes Mauriac's statement that "Thérèse Desqueyroux was myself," yet he fails to mention the Flaubertian echo in Mauriac's statement. The source of the quote, Claude Mauriac's *Le Temps immobile*, 234, is furnished by Jean Lacouture, p. 227, note 1. For more on this source, see Jean Lacouture, *François Mauriac* (Paris: Seuil, 1980), 206-211.
2. Bernard Pochmann, *Penance and the Anointing of the Sick*, trans., Francis Courtney (New York: Herder and Herder, 1964), 253.
3. Appendix C is devoted to a study of the parodic in Flaubert's *Un coeur simple*.
4. Joseph Wuest, *Matters Liturgical*, tr. Thomas Mullaney (New York and Cincinnati: Frederick Pustet , 1956), 719.
5. *The Catholic Encyclopedia* (New York: Robert Appleton, 1909), 5: 716.
6. *The New Catholic Encyclopedia* (New York: McGraw-Hill, 1967), 1: 571.
7. The section in Chapter 2 above on "Sexual Ambiguity in Mauriac's *Thérèse Desqueyroux*" further explores this dominant theme of ambiguity
8. Alison Fairlie, Flaubert: *Madame Bovary* (London: Edward Arnold, 1969), 29.
9. Dominick LaCapra, *Madame Bovary on Trial* (Ithaca and London: Cornell U. P., 1982), 55
10. Albert Thibaudet, *Gustave Flaubert* (Paris: Gallimard, 1935), 112-113.
11. Gérard Gengembre, *Gustave Flaubert: Madame Bovary* (Paris: P. U. F., 1990), 102.
12. Pierre Pierrard has published two studies on the rural curate in nineteenth-century France: *Du Prêtre français au XIXe siècle, 1801-1905* (Paris: Hachette, 1986) and, especially, *Histoire des curés de campagne de 1789 à nos jours* (Paris: Plon, 1986), where Chapter IV is entitled "Le curé en son village au temps du roi-bourgeois (1830-1848)."
13. In fact, one of the few books on Flaubert's religion, Suzanne Toulet's *Le Sentiment religieux de Flaubert d'après la correspondance* (Québec: Editions Cosmos, 1970), devotes a brief chapter to the author's anticlericalism (33-38) with only a passing reference to Bournisien (35).
14. A sampling of articles devoted to Homais would include the following: André Bourgeois, "M. Homais, instrument du destin," *South Central Review* 28 (1968): 124-126; Robert J. Niess, "On Listening to Homais," *French Review* 51 (1977): 22-28; Ulrich Schulz-Buschaus, "Homais oder die Norm des fortschrittlichen Berufsburgers: Zur Interpretation von Flauberts *Madame Bovary*," *Romanistisches Jahrbuch* 28 (1977): 126-149; James Rhodes, "Homais, Capharnaüm, and *Madame Bovary*, *College English* 10, no. 1 (1983): 60-68; and Michel Crouzet, "Ecce Homais," *Revue d'Histoire Littéraire de la France* 89, no. 6 (1989): 980-1014. Léon Bopp, in his book-length *explication de texte* of the novel, *Commentaire sur Madame Bovary* (Neuchâtel and Paris: La Baconnière, 1951), does discuss Bournisien *passim*. Mary Orr, in one of her recent books on Flaubert, *Madame Bovary: Representations of the Masculine*, (Bern: Peter Lang, 1999), does de-

vote a chapter (47-61) to Bournisien whose personality she views much more sympathetically than I.

15. Rosemary Lloyd, *Madame Bovary* (London: Unwin Hyman, 1990), 35, offers an interesting interpretation of Bournisien's entrance: "The priest's arrival at the inn is presented in terms parodic of the gothic novel, for the narrative eye, as if briefly incapable of interpreting the social significance of Bournisien's garb, records at first merely a man clad in black, whose sudden appearance makes the innkeeper shudder. But whatever the suggestions conjured up by Death come to summon his own, they are mockingly swept away by his rosy face, his athletic figure and the absent-mindedness that has caused him to forget his umbrella."

16. For other examples of the lack of narrative certainty in the novel, see the preceding note and the first section of the next chapter on "Narrative Uncertainty in *Madame Bovary*."

17. See Flaubert, *Le Dictionnaire des idées reçues*, in *Oeuvres complètes* (Paris: Seuil, 1964), 2: 313.

18. For examples of such pastoral cases involving the intersection of medicine, superstition, and religion among the peasantry in early nineteenth-century France, see Pierrard, *Histoire des curés de campagne*, 128-131.

19. Flaubert, *Correspondance* (Paris: Conard, 1926), 3: 166-167. The passage from the author's letter to Louise Colet is quoted by, among others, Fairlie, 8. The imperial prosecutor, Ernest Pinard, in his denunciation of the novel during the 1857 obscenity trial describes Bournisien, in words remarkably similar to Flaubert's own, as: "... prêtre à peu près aussi grotesque que le pharmacien, ne croyant qu'aux souffrances physiques, jamais aux souffrances morales, à peu près matérialiste" (500).

20. Bournisien's absence may be explained by the marked hostility of a large segment of the rural clergy to the July monarchy of Louis-Philippe; see Pierrard, *Histoire des curés de campagne*, 145-147.

21. Emma's father, rushing to Yonville in response to Homais' ambiguous letter following Emma's death, makes similar bargains with heaven: "... il promit à la sainte Vierge trois chasubles pour l'église, et qu'il irait pieds nus depuis le cimetière des Bertaux jusqu'à la chapelle de Vassonville" (429).

22. J.-L. Prévost, in *Le Prêtre, ce héros du roman* (Paris: Téqui, 1953), sees anger as a quality: "Les deux adversaires sont aussi stupides l'un que l'autre. L'abbé marque toutefois ... une supériorité sur son adversaire, c'est qu'il se défend avec une certaine bonhomie et sans jamais injurier personne. Irrité, il préfère s'en aller" (42).

23. Prévost defends Bournisien in spite of everything. "... l'auteur de *Madame Bovary*, en demandant tout au prêtre, n'a pas su voir ce qu'un simple curé de campagne pouvait donner à ses ouailles, malgré ses insuffisances" (43).

CHAPTER IV

Novel Uncertainties

Narrative Uncertainty in *Madame Bovary*

In his excellent study *The Perpetual Orgy: Flaubert and Madame Bovary*,[1] the Peruvian novelist Mario Vargas Llosa demonstrates incontrovertibly the preponderance of dualities in Flaubert's novel of provincial life. Most readers of the novel have noticed that characters, objects, and places often have doubles. Emma takes two lovers, Charles marries twice. Homais, the self-satisfied pharmacist and deist, spars frequently, as we have just seen, with his nemesis, the dim and insensitive curate Bournisien. Both Emma and Charles give away five franc pieces: she as a *beau geste* to the blind man, he into the collection basket during her funeral Mass. The ball at La Vaubyessard is replicated for Emma during the parodic visit of the organ grinder whose instrument is surmounted by a miniature ballroom featuring simian dancers. And the list of bipartite items could go on and on.[2]

Characters often demonstrate paired traits. Flaubert presents his characters not as one, but two; not unified, but as multivalent personalities. The effect is at times comic. Charles's father "avait l'aspect d'un brave, avec l'entretien facile d'un commis voyageur" (25). Flaubert describes the tenor Lagardy's personality as one "où il y avait du coiffeur et du toréador" (295). At times though this duality of personality more importantly underscores the disorder brought on by adultery, as when Emma, in her secret affair with Rodolphe, is made to play a double role: "... tout en faisant l'épouse et la vertueuse, elle s'enflammait à l'idée de cette tête ... et disposait son appartement et sa personne comme une courtisane qui attend un prince" (250).

On the narrative level as well, one finds, what I shall call, a duality of uncertainty in the description of characters' motives. This not infrequently invoked duality seems to have escaped the notice of most critics.[3] Now, there is nothing particularly unusual about a passage like this one, where Charles's mixed motivation paralyses him at the opera when Emma and Léon want to leave before the final scenes. Asked if he too is bored, Charles replies: "Oui ... peut-être ... un peu, ... indécis entre la franchise de son plaisir et le respect qu'il portait aux opinions de sa femme" (300).

There are, though, no fewer than fifteen instances in the novel where the narrator offers two possible motivations for a character's feelings or actions, without being able, it seems, to say which is the actual cause. Not surprisingly, the majority of these passages, nine in number, describe Emma, four Charles, and two Léon. These are, not coincidentally, the three least lucid characters who, in effect, least know themselves, are least conscious of their motives, and are least likely to plumb the wellsprings of their actions. All fifteen passages contain the conjunction *ou* or *ou bien* or the adverb *peut-être*, and quite frequently, the highly speculative *ou peut-être*. The narrative voice here becomes tentative and unsure, unable to penetrate the psyches of these characters, and so offers two possible explanations for their actions, words, or feelings.[4] Here follow the passages in question:

Léon 1: Speaking with Emma after the opera in Rouen, Léon tells her he was bored while studying law in Paris: "Pour se faire valoir, *ou* par une imitation naïve de cette mélancolie qui provoquait la sienne, le jeune homme déclara s'être ennuyé prodigieusement tout le temps de ses études" (307).[5]

Léon 2: Later, waylaid by the pharmacist and so unable to keep his planned rendez-vous with Emma at the Hôtel de Boulogne: "Léon, étourdi par la colère d'Emma, le bavardage de Monsieur Homais et *peut-être* les pesanteurs du déjeuner, restait indécis et comme sous la fascination du pharmacien...." (365-366).

Charles 1: Charles frequently lacks self-awareness and in this passage, were he to have thought why he returns to Les Bertaux the day after setting Monsieur Rouault's leg (which he does not), he might have proffered either one of these two possible, but wholly inapplicable, explanations: "Y eût-il songé, qu'il aurait sans doute attribué son zèle à la gravité du cas, *ou peut-être* au profit qu'il en espérait" (39).

Charles 2: The banality and the hollowness of Charles's personality are reinforced by the narrator who comments in this way on the *officier de santé*'s answer to Homais' question about whether an outing to the theatre might speed Emma's convalescence: "Sans doute, répondit le médecin nonchalamment, soit que, ayant les mêmes idées, il voulût n'offenser personne, *ou bien* qu'il n'eût pas d'idées" (289).

Charles 3: Charles's feelings after Emma's funeral Mass and burial are presented thus: "On l'emmena; et il ne tarda pas à s'apaiser, éprouvant *peut-être* comme tous les autres, la vague satisfaction d'en avoir fini" (433).

Charles 4: And finally, Charles does not rummage through Emma's desk after her death: "Par respect *ou* par une sorte de sensualité qui lui faisait mettre de la lenteur dans ses investigations, Charles n'avait pas encore ouvert le compartiment secret d'un bureau de pallisandre dont Emma se servait habituellement" (443).

Emma 1-9: Flaubert most often uses this strategy of narrative uncertainty in describing Emma. The author thus is able stylistically to reinforce his heroine's persistent lack of self-awareness and of lucidity. Consider the following nine passages:

1) Here is why she thought she had loved Charles after meeting him and even during the first days of their married life together: "Mais l'anxiété d'un état nouveau, *ou peut-être* l'irritation causée par la présence de cet homme, avait suffi à lui faire croire qu'elle possédait enfin cette passion merveilleuse" (68).

2) In resisting her passion for Léon: "Ce qui la retenait, sans doute, c'était la paresse *ou* l'épouvante, et la pudeur aussi" (152).

3) Before her planned flight to Italy with Rodolphe, Emma is obsequious to Charles and to her mother-in-law whom she loathes: "Etait-ce enfin de les mieux duper l'un et l'autre? *ou bien* voulait-elle, par une sorte de stoïcisme voluptueux, sentir plus complètement l'amertume des choses qu'elle allait abandonner!" (257).

4) There is no mention of her daughter as she and Rodolphe discuss their illicit flight to Italy: "Rodolphe évitait d'en parler, *peut-être* qu'elle n'y pensait pas" (261).

5) Most imprudently, Emma speaks of a former lover to Léon: "Un jour qu'ils causaient philosophiquement des illusions terrestres, elle vint à dire (pour expérimenter sa jalousie, *ou* cédant *peut-être* à un besoin d'épanchement trop fort) qu'autrefois, avant lui, elle avait aimé quelqu'un...." (351).[6]

6) Emma cannot bring herself to break off her affair with Léon even after she has tired of him: "Mais comment s'en débarrasser? Puis, elle avait beau se sentir humiliée de la bassesse d'un tel bonheur, elle y tenait par habitude *ou* par corruption...." (376).

7) Flaubert describes the feelings which take hold of Emma when she learns that all her possessions are to be seized to satisfy the enormous debts she has incurred: "Puis, quand ses yeux se reportaient sur la cheminée garnie d'écrans chinois, sur les larges rideaux, sur les fauteuils, sur toutes ces choses enfin qui avaient adouci l'amertume de sa vie, un remords la prenait, *ou* plutôt un regret immense, et qui irritait sa passion, loin de l'anéantir" (383).

8) Shortly after having repulsed Guillaumin's advances (with the grand retort "Je suis à plaindre, mais pas à vendre!"), Emma then considers a number of other possible actions: "L'envie lui vint de retourner chez Lheureux: à quoi bon? d'écrire à son père: il était trop tard; et *peut-être* qu'elle se repentait maintenant de n'avoir pas cédé à l'autre [Guillaumin], lorsqu'elle entendit le trot d'un cheval dans l'allée" (393-394).

9) Finally, Emma reacts to Rodolphe's mendacious explanation of why he had abandoned her: "Elle se laissa prendre à ses paroles, plus encore à sa voix et par le spectacle de sa personne; si bien qu'elle fit semblant de croire, *ou crut-*

elle *peut-être*, au prétexte de leur rupture; c'était un secret d'où dépendaient l'honneur et même la vie d'une troisième personne" (399).

In each of these fifteen passages, Flaubert uses an uncertain narrative voice which suggests several possible authorial stances. One can never fully understand one's own motivations nor totally explain one's feelings. And it is certainly true that Emma, Charles, and Léon, of all the characters in the novel, least understand, and, in fact, least try to understand themselves. To underscore, as well, that one cannot always or fully understand the motivations or the feelings of others either, Flaubert presents his often omniscient narrator as at a loss from time to time to fathom or even identify accurately the motives which prompt the behavior of the novel's three most romantic characters.

The novelist-critic Mario Vargas Llosa, in fact, identifies several distinct narrators in *Madame Bovary*: the plural narrator-character, the omniscient narrator, the invisible narrator, the philosopher narrator, and the single character-narrator.[7] Yet even he does not exhaust the subject, for in two memorable scenes the narrator withdraws from the main action being recounted in order both to preserve decorum and to suggest rather than to describe what precisely the characters are doing. The distanced narrator of the celebrated carriage ride, which Léon and Emma take after leaving the cathedral, conveys clearly though what is actually happening in the carriage. The "fureur de locomotion," the rhythmic thumping of the carriage, and the sight of the naked hand thrust out the window, all tell of the prolonged seduction and sexual surrender. Later, after the foreclosure and before the imminent seizure of the Bovarys' property, Emma is observed in a pantomime scene by two townswomen as she pleads with Binet for a loan. The less than certain nature of this scene is resolved by the women who conclude that Emma's hand on Binet's knee can only denote her offer to him of her sexual favors. In this scene, the voyeuristic narrative point of view causes the reader to remain less certain, and not absolutely sure of the precise nature of Emma's stance during her visit to the tax collector. Yet following, as this scene does, the narrator's uncertainty about whether Emma regretted not having yielded to Guillaumin's advances (see number 8 above), the reader may well come around to the townswomen's reading of the scene. Or perhaps the reader will not.

While the question of narration in Flaubert's novel is, then, an admittedly complex and hotly debated one, from this study of one of Flaubert's narrative strategies in *Madame Bovary*, we may now add yet another narrative voice, that of the uncertain narrator.

"Elle se penche sur sa propre énigme:"
Thérèse Desqueyroux, a Novel of Uncertainties

In the days leading up to her marriage to Bernard Desqueyroux, the feeling which Thérèse Larroque takes for peace, the narrator, who intervenes to correct the erroneous conclusion of his eponymous heroine, sees as something much more sinister:

> Jamais Thérèse ne connut une telle paix, —ce qu'elle croyait être la paix et qui n'était que le demi-sommeil, l'engourdissement de ce reptile dans son sein. (34)

Yet even this traditional and seemingly omniscient narrator, at other times, admits to not knowing for certain why characters act as they do or what characters think. Most of these examples deal with characters other than the central character, Thérèse, whose own uncertainties about her ability to create a coherent narrative for her husband underpin much of this short novel.

In the very first chapter, Mauriac's narrator, like Flaubert's uncertain narrator, offers two quite different, possible reasons for a question her lawyer asks Thérèse:

> Alors l'avocat, perfidement peut-être, —ou pour que Thérèse ne s'éloignât pas, sans qu'il lui eût adressé une parole, demanda si elle rejoignait dès ce soir M. Bernard Desqueyroux. (18)

Bernard's step-father, Victor de la Trave, reacts with unexpected, nostalgic irony to his wife's proposal to take their love-sick daughter Anne with them on a vacation trip in order to distract her during her forced separation from Jean Azévédo. Yet the narrator admits to not knowing the youthful event which M. de la Trave might be recalling:

> "Oh! un voyage avec nous.... Rien! rien!" répondait-il à sa femme qui, un peu sourde, l'interrogeait: "Qu'est-ce que tu as dit?" Du fond de cette fortune où il avait fait son trou, quel voyage d'amour se rappelait ce vieil homme, soudain, quelles heures bénies de sa jeunesse amoureuse? (48)

After Clara's death, the narrator can only suppose what Bernard's reaction to this unexpected, yet, for his purposes, not inconvenient loss may be: "Il a dû se dire que cet accident venait à point, ferait diversion" (90).

Now, all these examples of narrative uncertainty may simply be considered rhetorical devices used to suggest possible motives or events without having to furnish any details which would in all likelihood be superfluous. Nonetheless, uncertainty is not limited to these few passages. Rather it is surely the operative word one ought to use to describe the heroine's efforts to make sense of and to communicate her own past. Thérèse's own not infrequent modifications, reformulations, and her ultimate rejection of her story infuse the novel with an aura of irresolvable uncertainty. Can we know the motives of our own acts, can one adequately explain in a narrative construct what one did and why? The enigma that is Thérèse Desqueyroux herself—"Elle se penche sur sa propre énigme...." (46)—derives in large part from what the reader comes to see more and more clearly as Thérèse's inability to judge correctly and to narrate accurately. Much of the novel is devoted to her preparing her own story for Bernard after her acquittal for attempted murder. In the end, the long, worked-on story does not hold together at all. Then in the final chapters of the novel, her subsequent attempts to understand herself and her acts also prove futile, for narrative serves primarily as a reflection of psychology and psychologically Thésèse Desqueyroux's is a starkly bifurcated personality. All of these complications become clear only in the last few pages of the novel.

The first eight chapters of this novel chronicle Thérèse's preparation of the story of her act—her failed attempt to poison Bernard. The story is intended for her victim whose complicity in hiding her crime at trial assured her acquittal. Bernard had himself constructed another story in order to save Thérèse, that of his inadvertence in failing to pay attention as he took his heart medicine, the arsenic-based Fowler drops. His untruthful narrative bolsters Thérèse's even more mendacious and unlikely defense, that the forged prescription which she had taken to the pharmacist had been given to her by a needy worker from a neighboring farm, a man unseen by anyone else and unknown to all.

Unlike the narrator's claim in Balzac's *Le père Goriot* that "all is true," these two stories, and indeed many others, in Mauriac's novel prove in the end, all of them, not to be true or, at least, not to be at all convincing. Anne's perception and her description to Thérèse of the intense nature of Anne's relationship with Jean Azévédo does not at all match the young man's own version of their, for him, casual liaison. Madame de la Trave explains her daughter-in-law's reasons for marrying Bernard, yet these are undercut by Thérèse's retrospective analysis of her own motives, which themselves are far from clear. Even Thérèse's recollection of her wedding night is recalled first in one way, then immediately revised: "Thérèse, songeant à la nuit qui vint ensuite, murmure: 'Ce fut horrible....' puis se reprend: 'Mais non ... pas si horrible....'" (36). The narrative ground shifts constantly in this novel.

Even general observations about types of literary characters in novels appear to contradict each other. The narrator describes Thérèse seated alone in the first-class carriage of the train and declares her story to be more fascinating than any literary creation:

Impossible de lire: mais quel récit n'eût paru fade à Thérèse, au prix de sa vie terrible? Peut-être mourrait-elle de honte, d'angoisse, de remords, de fatigue, —mais elle ne mourrait pas d'ennui. (24)

This fictional character Thérèse, just described by the narrator as more exceptional than any character in a novel, later states her own tastes in literature. She rejects extraordinary and exceptional characters as utterly lacking in verisimilitude: "Elle exécrait dans les romans les peintures d'êtres extraordinaires et tels qu'on n'en rencontre jamais dans la vie" (54).

Thérèse does at times find some of the men in her own life to be extraordinary, yet in the final analysis none really is, in fact, all that exceptional. Having once thought that "le seul homme supérieur qu'elle crût connaître, c'était son père" (54), she now readjusts her view of him: "Mais si de loin, elle se faisait de lui une image embellie, Thérèse, dès qu'il était là, mesurait sa bassesse" (55). She then recalls her initial reaction to Jean Azévédo at her first meeting with him:

Cette avidité d'un jeune animal, cette intelligence dans un seul être, cela me paraissait si étrange que je l'écoutais sans l'interrompre. Oui décidément, j'étais éblouie.... (59)

But once again, further on in this recollection, she corrects her first impression:

En effet, il projetait dans le débat des clartés qui me paraissaient admirables.... Etaient-elles en somme si admirables?... Je crois bien que je vomirais aujourd'hui ce ragoût. (59)

And the local curate, "différent des autres," is for her a man who "avait pris un parti tragique; à la solitude intérieure, il avait ajouté ce désert que crée la soutane autour de l'homme qui la revêt" (70). But when she sees him at Sunday Mass after Clara's death, she describes him as devoid of any transcendent importance at all: "... entre deux enfants, un homme déguisé est debout, chuchotant, les bras un peu écartés" (91).

The key point which Thérèse hopes to explain to Bernard is why she tried to kill him. Early in her examination of conscience, however, her ability to explain herself is thrown into question when she admits the inauthenticity of her own unflattering portrait of Bernard:

Thérèse sourit à cette caricature de Bernard qu'elle dessine en esprit: "Au vrai, il était plus fin que la plupart des garçons que j'eusse pu épouser." (29)

And again:

> Que sais-je de Bernard, au fond? N'y a-t-il pas en lui infiniment plus que cette caricature dont je me contente, lorsqu'il faut me le représenter? (60)

So from the start, even she admits her inability to decipher and evaluate others, as she sets out to describe and explain herself.

Thérèse expends enormous energy preparing her *apologia* for Bernard. Yet at the very outset her own skepticism about the possibility of self-knowledge is clearly stated. Two passages in the second chapter of the novel suffice to support this conclusion. Having decided to tell all to Bernard, Thérèse feels "une sorte de desserrement délicieux: 'Bernard saura tout, je lui dirai....'" (23). But not knowing what she will say, she stops short and she acknowledges the impotence of words and the inaccessibility of knowledge of the self:

> Que lui dirait-elle? Par quel aveu commencer? Des paroles suffisent-elles à contenir cet enchaînement confus de désirs, de résolutions, d'actes imprévisibles? Comment font-ils tous ceux qui connaissent leurs crimes?... "Moi, je ne connais pas mes crimes. Je n'ai pas voulu celui dont on me charge. Je ne sais pas ce que j'ai voulu." (23)

Having reassured herself that a detailing of the facts "d'étape en étape" (24) should prove efficacious, she again falters:

> "Ah! songe Thérèse, il n'aura pas compris. Il faudra tout reprendre depuis le commencement...." Où est le commencement de nos actes? Notre destin, quand nous voulons l'isoler, ressemble à ces plantes qu'il est impossible d'arracher avec toutes leurs racines. Thérèse remontera-t-elle à son enfance? Mais l'enfance est elle-même une fin, un aboutissement. (25)

Along with the evocation of this striking image of the tenacious roots, resistant to exposure, which remain hidden and beyond our grasp, Thérèse, later during her confrontation with Bernard when he concludes that she did what she did in order to inherit his pine trees, in a statement reminiscent of La Rochefoucauld's image of motivations hidden in "tous les replis du coeur,"[8] compares the complex reality of her act and Bernard's judgment of it: "Entre les mille ressources de son acte, cet imbécile n'a donc su en découvrir aucune; et il invente la cause la plus basse...." (83). In spite of all her attempts to narrate, it is only while sequestered at Argelouse, and solely in her fantasy life, that she becomes a successful fabulator, as she imagines herself in Paris:

> Elle enchantait un cercle de visages attentifs, mais nullement étonnés. Une femme disait: "C'est comme moi ... j'ai éprouvé cela, moi aussi ...." Un homme de lettres la prenait à part: "Vous devriez écrire tout ce qui se passe en vous. Nous publierons ce journal d'une femme d'aujourd'hui dans notre revue." (95)

Thérèse's recollection of specific events in her own life and her recall or revisioning of them reveal to the reader a very unsure narrator whose perceptions, despite her often-cited intellectual acumen, are frequently exposed as erroneous.[9] Consider one part of her story, the most crucial: the trajectory of Bernard's illness. This part of Chapter 8 begins with a sentence suggesting that Thérèse will consider what she did in a direct, unmediated, forthright way: "La voici au moment de regarder en face l'acte qu'elle a commis" (73). In her recollection of a distracted Bernard adding a second dose of arsenic-based drops into his glass, Thérèse is portrayed as totally passive; aware, but unable to react. Minutes later, Bernard returns to the table after getting the news that the forest fire presents no threat to their trees and he takes yet another dose, a third, in fact, of his medication. Thérèse remains mute:

> Il demande: "Est-ce que j'ai pris mes gouttes?" et sans attendre la réponse, de nouveau, il en fait tomber dans son verre. Elle s'est tue par paresse *sans doute*, par fatigue. Qu'espère-t-elle à cette minute? "Impossible que j'aie prémédité de me taire." (73, my emphasis)

Sans doute! Perhaps! Yet that evening when the doctor is called to treat Bernard's retching and asks the family about his behavior that day, "... elle ne dit rien de ce qu'elle avait vu à table" (74). Even though she admits to herself that she could have mentioned the possibility of an accidental overdose in the midst of the day's confusion, "[e]lle demeura muette.... " (74).

From that day on, it is Thérèse who continues the slow poisoning of her husband. She matter-of-factly explains her act as the result of simple curiosity: "Oui, je n'avais pas du tout le sentiment d'être la proie d'une tentation horrible; il s'agissait d'une curiosité un peu dangereuse à satisfaire" (74). Her only "slightly" dangerous curiosity thereafter becomes a totally overwhelming force, and one fully beyond the control of a woman described, with insistent repetition, in the passive voice: "... elle s'est engouffrée dans le crime béant; elle a été aspirée par le crime" (74). Subsequently, all she recalls are Bernard's periodically worsening symptoms, described by her as if she were an objective, disinterested observer rather than as an actor. Even as Bernard is finally taken to the hospital in Bordeaux, Thérèse still is not identified as the poisoner, but only metaphorically as a hunted animal who hears the pack of dogs nearby and as a runner who falters in sight of the finish-line:

> Thérèse était demeurée à Argelouse; mais quelle que fût sa solitude, elle percevait autour d'elle une immense rumeur, bête tapie qui entend se rapprocher la meute; accablée comme après une course forcenée, —comme si, tout près du but, la main tendue déjà, elle avait été soudain précipitée à terre, les jambes rompues. (76)

Lynn Kettler Penrod explains in her study of the function of focalization in Mauriac's novel how "this particular insistence on limited vision"—with Thérèse as the principal character-focalizer—"contributes to the general reader sympathy generated for the character Thérèse."[10] The reader views her role as she would see it herself: as passive, rather than as continually active, effective, and just this side of deadly.

Thérèse, in fact, manages in the final chapters of the novel to pass herself off as the victim. The deprivation throughout her long sequestration too arouses readers' sympathy—and even Bernard's! He returns after weeks away to find a gaunt, enfeebled Thérèse whose appearance triggers in his mind a childhood memory of a picture in a newspaper of the ill-treated and lamentable *Séquestrée de Poitiers*.[11] Thérèse never uses her well-prepared confession to explain herself to Bernard, for "Au vrai, cette histoire trop bien construite demeurait sans lien avec la réalité" (87); rather:

> Non, non: elle avait obéi à une profonde loi, à une loi inexorable; elle n'avait pas détruit cette famille, c'était elle qui serait donc détruite; ils avaient raison de la considérer comme un monstre, mais elle aussi les jugeait monstrueux. Sans que rien ne parût au dehors, ils allaient, avec cette lente méthode, l'anéantir. (87)

Without using the term, Thérèse claims here that she had acted in self-defense.[12]

In the novel's last chapter where the final conversation unfolds between the spouses at the Café de la Paix in Paris, Thérèse again thinks of her story, rejected long ago now, as Bernard asks her, in spite of himself, *Why?*:

> Cette confession longuement préparée, dans la victoria, au long de la route de Nizan, puis dans le petit train de Saint-Clair, cette nuit de recherches, cette quête patiente, cet effort pour remonter à la source de son acte, —enfin ce retour épuisant sur soi-même était peut-être au moment d'obtenir son prix. (110)

Yet even now, after all her ruminations and her long solitude at Argelouse, she is still unable to explain herself. At first she jokes and says naturally that it was because of her desire for his pine trees. Then she suggests it was to cause him some disquietude, to make him wonder and question. Bernard rejects this second explanation as another of her paradoxes: "Vous aurez donc de l'esprit jusqu'à la fin...." (110). Her third attempt at an answer takes the reader back to the theme of the impossibility of narrative when Thérèse tells him:

> —Moi, j'aurais tant voulu que rien ne vous demeurât caché. Si vous saviez à quelle torture je me suis soumise, pour voir clair.... Mais toutes les raisons que j'aurais pu vous donner, comprenez-vous, à peine les eussé-je énoncées, elles m'auraient paru menteuses.... (111)

He insists; she begins to recount the day of the fire, the first day of his mysterious illness. He laughs at her! And the narrator's parenthetical observation following Bernard's dismissive response again confirms the failure of communication or, indeed, even its possibility: "'Non, mais pour qui me prenez-vous?' Il ne la croyait pas (mais au vrai, ce qu'elle disait, était-ce croyable?)" (111).

Thérèse now judges herself harshly, positing for the first time the possibility of having premeditated her crime and the admission of an active, relentless, tenacious pursuit of her goal after Bernard's first accidental overdoses during the fire:

> Elle mit une passion étrange à se charger: pour avoir agi ainsi en somnambule, il fallait, à l'entendre, que, depuis des mois, elle eût accueilli dans son coeur, qu'elle eût nourri des pensées criminelles. D'ailleurs, le premier geste accompli, avec quelle fureur lucide elle avait poursuivi son dessein! avec quelle ténacité. (112)

Her statement of why she acted in this way is specific, but unexplained: "Je cédais à un affreux devoir. Oui, c'était comme un devoir" (112). Bernard, unconvinced, again asks *why*, what did she want? And it is only now that Thérèse sufficiently realizes the complex nature of her personality to begin haltingly to attempt to articulate a statement about its duality. She speaks of both the domestic Thérèse, the Thérèse protective of her pine forests and proud to be a Desqueyroux, or, as she says, "contente enfin de se caser" (113), on the one hand, and, on the other hand, the "other" Thérèse. Yet, having managed to identify these two parts of herself, when Bernard asks her "Quelle autre?" all we read is this sparse, but sadly evocative, sentence: "Elle ne sut que répondre...." (113).

Like Susanne Simonin, in Diderot's *La religieuse*, who, having suffered physically and psychologically for years in the convent she was forced to enter against her will, once free in Paris, but no better off, exclaims: "Si j'eusse été voisine de mon couvent, j'y retournais,"[13] so too Thérèse. Now about to be free to live in Paris, we read that: "Si Bernard lui avait dit: 'Je te pardonne; viens ...', elle se serait levée, l'aurait suivi" (114).[14] But even in these concluding paragraphs of the novel, contradiction and uncertainty dominate. No more than an hour later at the end of a solitary lunch in a café, Thérèse rejects the just-made, startling statement about her willingness to follow Bernard: "La route de Villandrut, le soir, entre les pins sinistres, dire qu'il y a une heure à peine, elle souhaitait de s'y enfoncer aux côtés de Bernard!" (115).[15]

Is it any wonder then that Thérèse remains enigmatic and that the nature of her motivations puzzles and frustrates readers and critics. As we saw in the second section of Chapter 2, Thérèse's sexuality is highly ambiguous. Similarly, her ideas too seem unstable, as they change to reflect, it seems, now one, now the other side of her split personality. Needing to sustain both of these two

Thérèses, she is unable to formulate a clear picture of a univocal personality, for she is not one person but two, and as such, it seems, she is doomed to unhappiness, responding now to the needs of the one Thérèse, at the expense of the other. Her seeming lucidity, her attempts to identify the motivations of her actions prove to be illusory. Narrative uncertainty reflects the instability of her personality, or to put it another way, its irreconcilable complexity. And so the haunting description of her final movement in the novel is mimetic of her lack of purpose, lack of focus, lack of wholeness: "... ayant gagné la rue, [elle] marcha au hasard" (115).

NOTES

1. New York: Farrar, Straus and Giroux, 1976.
2. See Vargas Llosa's section "The Binary World," 145-166, which contains an extensive, but not exhaustive, list of doublets. He does not, for example, mention the last pair, the ball and the organ grinder, which one could well consider key to understanding Emma's sense of depravation.
3. It was only after my section on narrative uncertainty appeared in article form that I discovered in a monograph by Tony Williams entitled *Psychological Determinism in Madame Bovary*, Occasional Papers in Modern Languages no. 9, (Hull: University of Hull Publications, 1973), 75-76, a passage where he writes first of the use of *peut-être* and *sans doute* at moments when Flaubert's narrator is "forced to hazard tentative remarks rather than provide hard and fast answers about motivations" (75). In my study, I have not considered passages like these in the novel. Williams does go on, though, to talk about times when "the narrator also 'thinks aloud' about motives" (75) and mentions three of the examples I have noted.
4. R. J. Sherrington (whose position Culler, see *infra*, summarizes and then refutes) takes the position in his *Three Novels by Flaubert* (Oxford: Oxford U. P., 1970) that the narrator in *Madame Bovary* is a shifting and unstable one. Sherrington (133) mentions Leo Bersani's postulation of yet another narrator: a "bourgeois narrator, a narrator who is almost a character, who reflects the base, collective mind of the community ...." Others considering this complex narrative question arrive at other conclusions. The most extreme perhaps is represented by Jonathan Culler in *Flaubert: The Uses of Uncertainty* (Ithaca: Cornell U. P., 1974), 112, who rejects Sherrington's view and declares that "the text is not narrated by anyone and ... the attempt to read it as if it were can lead only to confusion." Critics writing after the appearance of Culler's ground-breaking study offer views consonant with his. Consider, for example: Michal P. Ginsberg who writes this in her *Flaubert Writing: A Study in Narrative Strategies* (Stanford: Stanford U. P., 1986): "What characterizes *Madame Bovary* is not simply the existence of different narrators, but one's inability to pinpoint portions of the text as originating with a specific narrator. The source of the narration is undecidable, and instead of having multiple nar-

rators (each of which can still have a distinct identity), we have an "exploded" narrator who does not have a distinct set of characteristics and cannot therefore be opposed to another narrator, or to a character" (103). In his brief chapter entitled "A Narratological Approach to *Madame Bovary*," in *Approaches to Teaching Flaubert's Madame Bovary*, ed. Laurence Porter and Eugene Gray (New York: MLA, 1995), Gerald Prince speaks of Flaubertian "narrative indeterminacy" (85) and concludes that "the elusiveness of the narrator, the variability of voice, and the multiplication of viewpoints underlie the novel's brand of impersonality (and objectivity)" (86).

5. V. K. Ramazani discusses this passage (97) and the first passage dealing with Emma (59) in his study *The Free Indirect Mode: Flaubert and the Poetics of Irony* (Charlottesville: University Press of Virginia, 1988). In neither case, though, does he take note of the duality of motivation under discussion here.

6. Stirling Haig, in *Flaubert and the Gift of Speech: Dialogue and Discourse in Four Modern Novels* (Cambridge: Cambridge U. P., 1986), does comment on this passage: "Even the narrator refuses to vouch for Emma's motives in a parenthesis where he actually distances himself from her: is she playing the coquette, seeking to provoke her lover's jealousy, or does she yield to an indiscreet impulse?" (86). Haig's statement that here the narrator *actually* distances himself from Emma suggests that Haig sees this example as unique. In fact, the technique is, as I demonstrate, not infrequently utilized. On page 100, for example, when Haig studies Emma's final meeting with Rodolphe, containing the narrator's uncertainty ("... elle fit semblant de croire, ou crut-elle peut-être au prétexte de leur rupture;" see my ninth and final quote under "Emma"), he does not even reproduce and, therefore, does not in any way comment on this part of the scene. Rather, he uses ellipsis to cut it out from that part of the scene which he does study in detail.

7. See Vargas Llosa, 184-198.

8. François de La Rochefoucauld, *Réflexions ou Sentences et Maximes morales* (Paris, 1664), 486, uses the expression in a "Lettre de La Rochefoucauld au Père Thomas Esprit," 6 février 1664. This text, part of the Bibliopolis e-texts, is freely accessible and searchable on a site called Biblionet: <http://minotaure.bibliopolis.fr:7999/default.htm>

9. Critics of the novel have long seen the uncertainty of Thérèse's motivations as an integral part of her enigmatic personality. Jean Lacouture writes this compelling statement about her attempt on Bernard's life: "Que Thérèse, ni l'auteur, ni le lecteur ne puisse trouver de fondement à cet acte amorcé dans l'irrésolution, poursuivi dans l'inconscient et achevé dans l'incertitude, il y a là une vertu romanesque qui fait penser à Dostoïevski" (*François Mauriac*, Paris: Seuil, 1980, 216).

10. Lynn Kettler Penrod, "Focalization without (Too Much) Fuss: Using Narratology to Teach *Thérèse Desqueyroux*," *ADFL Bulletin* 19, no. 2 (1988): 10. Following Genette and others, she defines focalization succinctly as "who sees" (8). The ur-text on focalization remains that by Gérard Genette in *Figures III: discours du récit* (Paris: Seuil, 1972), 206-211. James Phelan alerts readers to the unsettled interpretation of Genette's term, in the first sentence of his recent article "Why Narrators Can Be Focalizers—and Why It Matters," 51-64, in *New Perspectives on Narrative Perspective*, ed. W. van Peer and Seymour Chatman (Albany: SUNY Press, 2001), where he writes: "... I want to take another look at the various concepts swirling around the term focalization and to propose a new way of thinking about the relation between the term and the concept" (51).

11. For a study of this criminal case from 1901 which Mauriac refers to in the novel, see Jean-Marie Augustin, *L'histoire véridique de la Séquestrée de Poitiers*, (Paris: Fayard, 2001). The following web-site also offers text and photos about the case: <http://sequestreedepoitiers.free.fr>

12. While James H. Reid does at times present interesting insights into the relationship between first- and third-person narration in the novel in his alliteratively-titled article "Mauriac: the Ambivalent Author of Absence," *Studies in Twentieth-Century Literature* 2 , no. 2 (1987): 167-188, at other times his presentation is rather more opaque. One of his conclusions, though tempting, is not supported by the text of the novel. Reid writes about Thérèse that "Since part of her wants to be an accomplice in the family's common destiny, she cannot explain her crime by saying that it was motivated by a need to eliminate the family's influence in her life" (174). The "*loi profonde*" (87) of her being and her "*affreux devoir*" (112) to which Thérèse refers undercut Reid's conclusion. She can and she does want to eliminate the family while, paradoxically, feeling a need to find refuge in its ranks.

13. Denis Diderot, *La religieuse* (Paris: Garnier-Flammarion, 1968), 198.

14. A comparison with Diderot's heroine is not at all that fanciful, for in an abandoned version of the novel (MS I), Mauriac had referred to Aunt Clara as a "vieille radicale qui a lu *la Religieuse* de Diderot.... " (see the notes to the edition of the novel in Mauriac's *Oeuvres romanesques et théâtrales complètes*, ed. Jacques Petit (Paris: Gallimard, 1979), 2: 965). Clara's watching the confrontation between Thérèse and Bernard through the keyhole in the door in Chapter 9 of the novel recalls Susanne's eavesdropping at the parlor door on the conversation between the abbess of Arpagon and her confessor, dom Morel.

15. Interestingly Jacques Petit, quoting Mauriac in the *Notice* to the novel in Vol. II, p. 927 of Petit's Pléiade edition (see previous note), underscores the primacy of forgiveness over self-knowledge: "'Le mouvement le plus profond du roman, plus que le désir de se comprendre, est peut-être un conflit entre le besoin d'être pardonné qui a toujours été en moi' dit Mauriac [*Ce que je crois*, 25] et une résistance plus forte que ce besoin. Double mouvement qui répond à la crise religieuse qu'il traverse alors."

CHAPTER V

Supporting Players

Undiscovered Countries: the Role of Some Minor Characters in *Madame Bovary*

One of the functions of secondary characters, and of minor ones as well, is to help realistic novelists flesh out their fictional worlds. Much has been written, for example, on Homais; much less, as we have seen, on Bournisien, the stalwart, but dull-witted, village priest. Binet, the tax collector, and even the blind beggar have attracted critical attention.[1]

Among his many minor characters, it is not those for whom Flaubert furnishes thumb-nail biographies—like Charles's parents or Emma's father—but rather those minor characters referred to in passing and whose lives are evoked only fleetingly, who impel the reader to imagine lives whose slim contours must be invented, practically *ex nihilo*.

At times, Emma herself engages in such inventions. The Vicomte with whom she waltzed at La Vaubyessard takes on in her mind an amorous life shared with a mistress and marked by gallant adventures, which spring entirely from the title character's imagination. At La Vaubyessard itself, after the ball has ended and unable to sleep, Emma yearns to know the lives of the other guests: "Elle regarda les fenêtres du château, longuement, tâchant de deviner quelles étaient les chambres de tous ceux qu'elle avait remarqués la veille. Elle aurait voulu savoir leurs existences, y pénétrer, s'y confondre" (85). In a similar way later in the novel, Emma creates her version of the tenor Lagardy's life story, and into it she insinuates herself by the sole force of her imagination.

Other characters enjoy no such internal, character-generated existences. It is rather the reader who must choose to imagine the lives of these characters who exist in Flaubert's text sometimes as little more than presences. These kinds of characters include not only the nameless hairdresser whose shop in Tostes faces

Emma's window, but slightly more developed ones like Justin, Homais' servant, and Madame Homais, both of whom also require or, at the very least, invite readers to imagine much of what they too feel and why. The function of all three of these characters as doubles for Charles or Emma, as well, becomes more obvious as the reader ponders the nature of their feelings. And we come again to yet more examples to bolster Mario Vargas Llosa's insistence on the preponderance of doubles in the novel.

The *perruquier* at Tostes, described but once in the novel, is one of several doubles who manifests in some way a life rather similar to Emma's. Her ennui at Tostes, after returning from La Vaubyessard, is palpable and crushing—"... elle ... sentait l'ennui plus lourd qui retombait sur elle" (97-98)—and her neighbor the hairdresser feels the same distress from an unfulfilled life:

> Lui aussi, le perruquier, il se lamentait de sa vocation arrêtée, de son avenir perdu, et, rêvant quelque boutique dans une grande ville, comme à Rouen, par exemple, sur le port, près du théâtre, il restait toute la journée à se promener en long, depuis la mairie jusqu'à l'église, sombre et attendant la clientèle. (98)

He has no name, no history, no other attributes than his boredom and his yearning. Like Emma, who dreams of La Vaubyessard and who knows only the visits of the organ-grinder whose waltzing simian puppets (98-99) make a mockery of her aspirations, the *perruquier*'s empty shop in Tostes, before which he paces, represents his entire reality, far from the dreamed-of thriving economy of Rouen with its port and theatres.

Emma will frequent just such a shop in Rouen, rue de la Comédie, on Thursdays after her weekly rendez-vous with Léon:

> Elle allait rue de la Comédie, chez un coiffeur, se faire arranger ses bandeaux. La nuit tombait; on allumait le gaz dans la boutique....
> Il faisait chaud dans ce petit appartement trop bas, où le poêle bourdonnait au milieu des perruques et des pommades. L'odeur des fers, avec ces mains grasses qui lui maniaient la tête, ne tardait pas à l'étourdir, et elle s'endormait un peu sous son peignoir. Souvent le garçon, en la coiffant, lui proposait des billets pour le bal masqué. (347-348)

Is there any certainty at all that a professional life like the one described here would, in fact, satisfy the *perruquier* of Tostes? Would this "petit appartement trop bas" really be such an improvement? The *perruquier*'s ennui may well be endemic and incurable, like Emma's, even should the sought-for goal be achieved. It does not take much effort to transfer the habitual dissatisfaction which recurs in Emma's life to the life of this other victim of *bovarysme*.

Justin, the serving lad, and Madame Homais, the pharmacist's wife, are more fully described than the *perruquier*. Yet, while we do know some things about them both, their inner feelings are either described ever so briefly or described not at all, but only suggested and then just faintly. While Justin is another Charles, deeply in love with Emma, yet always unnoticed and unappreciated by her, Madame Homais is, although the very palest shadow of the eponymous heroine, nonetheless another Emma, at least in that she like Emma is susceptible, it seems, to the charms of the handsome clerk Léon Dupuis.

Justin, a pharmacy student and distant cousin of Homais, has been taken in by the pharmacist who uses the lad as a domestic servant and general factotum. The youth serves Emma too, cleaning her shoes "tout empâtées de crotte—la crotte des rendez-vous—qui se détachait en poudre sous ses doigts, et qu'il regardait monter doucement dans un rayon de soleil" (251); inspiring her to covet a blue coach drawn by an English horse and driven by a groom; and hoping to be taken into her service as her *valet de chambre* (351). Is he too, like Emma, a reader of romantic literature? We know that his hormones are raging, for not only does he hover around Emma's maid Félicité as she irons her mistress's intimate garments, but after invading the pharmacist's *sanctum sanctorum* and taking a pot from next to the arsenic bottle, he is caught by Homais in possession of a book, an illicit one which falls from the young man's pocket, an illustrated book entitled, as read by Homais "en séparant lentement les deux mots: L'Amour ... conjugal" (327).

Long before this moment, Justin's passionate feeling for Emma had been made explicit to the reader in this scene where the feckless youth plays a voyeuristic role:

> ... il restait debout près de la porte, immobile, sans parler. Souvent même, Mme Bovary, n'y prenait garde, se mettait à sa toilette. Elle commençait par retirer son peigne, en secouant sa tête d'un mouvement brusque; et, quand il aperçut la première fois cette chevelure entière qui descendait jusqu'aux jarrets en déroulant ses anneaux noirs, ce fut, pour lui, le pauvre enfant, comme l'entrée subite dans quelque chose d'extraordinaire et de nouveau dont la splendeur l'effraya.
>
> Emma, sans doute, ne remarquait pas ses empressements silencieux ni ses timidités. Elle ne se doutait point que l'amour, disparu de sa vie, palpitait là, près d'elle, sous cette chemise de grosse toile, dans ce coeur d'adolescent ouvert aux émanations de sa beauté. (285-286)

Like Charles, adoring Emma yet ever unable to understand her fatal unhappiness, Justin too contributes unknowingly to Emma's death, by alerting her to where in the capharnaüm Homais keeps the arsenic. Indeed, Justin is present as she swallows the poison, yet cannot stop her, just as Charles, the ineffectual *officier de santé*, once she has eaten the poison, cannot cure her:

> —Arrêtez! s'écria-t-il en se jetant sur elle.

—Tais-toi! on viendrait....
Il se désespérait, voulait appeler.
—N'en dis rien; tout retomberait sur ton maître! (405)

The night of Emma's burial is the last time we see Justin, and, although he is not even named, the reader is well aware of who is being described. Justin, unlike both Léon and Rodolphe, each of whom is fast asleep, keeps watch at her grave:

> Il y avait un autre qui, à cette heure-là, ne dormait pas.
> Sur la fosse, entre les sapins, un enfant pleurait agenouillé, et sa poitrine, brisée par les sanglots, haletait dans l'ombre, sous la pression d'un regret immense, plus doux que la lune et plus insondable que la nuit. (435)

Flaubert interrupts the melancholic scene and concludes this paragraph, and thus the chapter, with a typically abrupt change of tone. The romantic Justin—recognized by the gravedigger—is frightened off, his very presence terribly misunderstood by the practical Lestiboudois, who himself profits from every occasion, and who is clearly incapable of imagining any reason but the following to explain the youth's nocturnal visit to the graveyard:

> La grille tout à coup craqua. C'était Lestiboudois; il venait chercher sa brêche qu'il avait oubliée tantôt. Il reconnut Justin escaladant le mur, et sut alors à quoi s'en tenir sur le malfaiteur qui lui dérobait ses pommes de terre. (435)

Just as Bernard Desqueyroux can posit Thérèse's desire to possess his pine trees as the only plausible motive for her attempt on his life, Lestiboudois, who digs graves and grows potatoes in the richly fertilized soil of the graveyard, thus, according to the curate, profiting twice from the dead, can imagine no other reason for Justin's nocturnal visit to the cemetery that the theft of his illicit tubers. Yet even Lestiboudois' cynicism cannot diminish the beauty and intensity of the young man's adoration of Emma and the pathos of this final moment near her.

Flaubert creates an even more poignant example of the minor character whose inner feelings are not even so clearly elaborated as Justin's, but rather just hinted at, in Madame Homais. Like her spouse the pharmacist, she has no first name. In an echo of the novel's title, she is known only by the honorific due her marital status followed by her husband's family name. We do know that she dresses the children against the cold in swaddle which alarms even Homais, so tightly are their heads wrapped (162-163). She loves to eat *cheminots*, Norman Lenten rolls, a survival of medieval tastes (386). And according to, of all people, Emma, who scolds Léon for deprecating the woman, she is quite simply "une bonne mère de famille" (150).

For Léon, overcome with ennui, who passes in mental review all those among whom he lives, and for us readers too, the shadowy Madame Homais stands for bourgeois maternal devotion. Léon's reflections on her—both positive and negative—become perforce our view of her too:

> Quant à la femme du pharmacien, c'était la meilleure épouse de Normandie, douce comme un mouton, chérissant ses enfants, son père, sa mère, ses cousins [note there is no mention of *son mari*], pleurant aux maux d'autrui, laissant tout aller dans son ménage, et détestant les corsets;—mais si lente à se mouvoir, si ennuyeuse à écouter, d'un aspect si commun et d'une conversation si restreinte, qu'il n'avait jamais songé quoiqu'elle eût trente ans et qu'il en eût vingt, qu'ils couchassent porte à porte, et qu'il lui parlât chaque jour, qu'elle pût être une femme pour quelqu'un, ni qu'elle possédât de son sexe autre chose que la robe. (137)

Yet at Léon's departure from Yonville for Paris, Flaubert presents not only Emma's reaction but Madame Homais' as well—and each with the same minimalist technique which causes us to see both of these two so very different women as really quite similar in their loss. We are fully aware of Emma's barely controlled and contained passion for the young clerk. It becomes clear that Madame Homais' feelings for him are intense too.

Emma listens silently to Homais' long disquisition on the dangers for provincials like Léon which the capital presents. Through it all, Flaubert allows Emma but two subtle movements. He describes not her thoughts or her feelings, but her physical reactions only: "Madame Bovary soupira" (168) and, a bit farther on, "Emma tressaillit" (169).

Madame Homais' reaction at Léon's departure is remarkably similar: no words, just an attitude reported by her husband. As Homais arrives at the Bovarys', Charles asks him: "—Et quoi de neuf chez vous?" To which the pharmacist replies:

> —Pas grand-chose. Ma femme, seulement, a été, cette après-midi, un peu émue. Vous savez, les femmes, un rien les trouble! la mienne surtout! Et l'on aurait tort de se révolter là contre, puisque leur organisation nerveuse est beaucoup plus malléable que la nôtre. (168)

Both Emma and Madame Homais are moved, and deeply so, by the loss of Léon, whose elegance and charm enriched their dreary lives by his very presence in Yonville. Can one not reasonably conclude that Madame Homais, like Emma, was attracted to Léon, despite *his* inability even to imagine her as possessing anything more of her sex than the dresses she wore? Flaubert wrote to Louise Colet that "Ma pauvre Bovary, sans doute, souffre et pleure dans vingt villages de France à la fois, à cette heure même."[2] The author suggests in this letter of 14 August 1853 that Emma is surely not alone in her longing for love and for something more than conjugal banality with the likes of Charles. Not only in the provincial back-waters of France, but in the very novel itself, Flaubert includes Madame Homais as yet another example of the unhappily married woman longing silently for someone better, more dashing, more handsome, more refined, and more charming.

For Homais, his wife's indisposition is explained simply as another defect of female biology. For us, the depths of her dissatisfaction and the intensity of her desire for something better are clearly suggested by the fact that this particular afternoon she had become "un peu émue." The understatement of Homais' "un peu" and of his dismissive "un rien les trouble!" underscores, rather, a secret emotional life never perceived by Léon and, not surprisingly, totally beyond Homais' ken, just as Emma's sadness and dissatisfaction totally escape the myopic Charles.

Minor characters not only enrich the fictional landscape, then, suggesting other lives we will never fully know at all, but which we could, were the author willing to flesh them out, but their resonances with the major characters are also often of prime importance. The *perruquier* both echoes and highlights Emma's melancholy and ennui. The odd pair, Justin-Madame Homais, underscore for the reader the commonality of the feelings of both Charles and Emma. While this is the Bovarys' story, their feelings, respectively, of deep but blind devotion and unattainable yearning are not unique, but rather shared in other registers by others living quite quiet, yet quite intense, lives in their very midst. While Charles and Emma are indeed unique individuals, their feelings are in no way idiosyncratic. It is through certain of his minor characters that Flaubert makes this clear to us and further justifies the novel's subtitle: *moeurs de province*.

"Aussi réelle que l'autre:"
Alterity in *Thérèse Desqueyroux*

We recently marked the seventy-fifth anniversary of the publication of François Mauriac's *Thérèse Desqueyroux* and the work continues to intrigue and its characters continue to haunt readers' imaginations. If, as I tried to establish in the preceding section, a few minor characters serve as avatars for Emma and Charles Bovary, Flaubert's major players, an entire clan inhabits Mauriac's *Thérèse Desqueyroux*: a clan whose collective force of only slightly modulated conformity stands squarely in opposition to Thérèse, the title character. Her family is intolerant of her personality and intent on policing and punishing her activities. None of her relatives—except perhaps her mother-in-law—comes entirely devoid of some saving grace, some spark of humanity; yet each one also exhibits traits and habits which valorize the group and its hegemony and, consequently, enforce a denigration and an intolerance of individual difference and uniqueness.

Thérèse's father, Monsieur Larroque, and her mother-in-law, Madame de la Trave, while un-related, incarnate oppressive parental control of even their adult children, especially, and perhaps not surprisingly, their daughters. M. Larroque sees women as "toutes des hystériques quand elles ne sont pas des idiotes" (18 and 55) and insists on preserving the family's reputation and on advancing his political ambitions, at all costs. Similarly, Mme de la Trave has raised Bernard to remonstrate against whatever may threaten the good of the family and so he comes to repeat, like his father-in-law, a disdainful and self-satisfied dictum: "On n'est malheureux que par sa propre faute" (28 and 84).[3]

Bernard and his mother succeed finally in controlling Anne, Bernard's half-sister. Her infatuation with Jean Azévédo is ruthlessly thwarted, while her maternal and familial instincts are applauded. Toward the end of the novel, Anne too becomes a mouthpiece for the family as she condemns her former intimate Thérèse for being unmaternal:

> ... elle répétait souvent, avec les mêmes intonations que sa mère: "Je lui aurais tout pardonné, parce que, enfin, c'est une malade; mais son indifférence pour Marie, je ne peux pas la digérer. Une mère qui ne s'intéresse pas à son enfant, vous pouvez inventer toutes les excuses que vous voudrez, je trouve ça ignoble." (104)

Even the seemingly less intolerant Hector de la Trave, Anne's father and Bernard's step-father, though troubled by the harsh treatment Anne receives, acquiesces to the family's decision to frustrate Anne's desire to be with Azévédo. M. de la Trave, like Bernard and M. Larroque, speaks in maxims:

> "Tâchons de la [Anne] faire souffrir le moins possible ..." répétait Hector de la Trave; mais lui, qui naguère cédait aux plus absurdes caprices d'Anne, ne pouvait qu'approuver sa femme, disant: "On ne fait pas d'omelettes sans casser les oeufs ..." et encore: "Elle nous remerciera un jour." (47)

When his wife suggests a trip for Anne and them as a way of distancing their daughter from Jean, M. de la Trave thinks of his own youth:

> Du fond de cette fortune où il avait fait son trou, quel voyage d'amour se rappelait ce vieil homme, soudain, quelles heures bénies de sa jeunesse amoureuse? (48)

Here Mauriac obliquely, yet evocatively, suggests a past experience not unlike that yearned for by his daughter Anne. Not related to the Larroques or the Desqueyroux, except by marriage, M. de la Trave, while now compromised and thoroughly co-opted by what Thérèse will call "la famille maternelle et toute puissante" (87), has indulged, it seems apparent, in less than proper behavior himself.

Just as Aunt Clara's sexual frustration undercuts the seriousness of her anticlericalism, the old woman straddles the divide between acceptance of narrow family values and support for an individual like Thérèse. Like Anne who will marry lovelessly to unite the land holdings of two prominent families, Clara has accepted, not without great resentment, another traditional bourgeois role, that of the spinster. An insightful Thérèse understands Clara's personality: "... au fond (songeait Thérèse) plus croyante qu'aucun la Trave, mais en guerre ouverte contre l'Etre infini qui avait permis qu'elle fût sourde et laide, qu'elle mourût sans avoir jamais été aimée ni possédée" (55).[4] Bernard too, at the end of the novel, will accept the masculine role equivalent to Clara's spinsterly one: "Chaque génération de Desqueyroux a eu son vieux garçon! Il fallait bien que ce fût moi" (114).

Clara, upon the death of Thérèse's mother in childbirth while Thérèse herself was still "au berceau," served as a substitute mother for the motherless Thérèse.[5] It can hardly be considered a stretch to suppose that Thérèse decides to marry Bernard, in part at least, in order to avoid just such a fate as Clara's and one which Thérèse had observed since childhood. Unmarried and frustrated, cranky and complaining, Clara in her spinsterhood may well have been an ever-present reminder of the type of woman whom Thérèse, by marrying Bernard, wished to avoid becoming: "... elle voulait être rassurée contre elle ne savait quel péril" (33).[6]

Both Bernard and Thérèse's father stand as exemplars of traditional patriarchy and, as such, are presented by the author in the most unfavorable light, at least, usually. Mauriac does, however, suggest less caricatured beings when Thérèse, their sole critic, proffers positive, though qualified, evaluations of these men. Thérèse, early on, describes certain virtues hidden under Bernard's rough exterior:

> Sous la dure écorce de Bernard n'y avait-il une espèce de bonté? Lorsqu'il était tout près de mourir, les métayers disaient: "Après lui, il n'y aura plus de monsieur, ici." Oui, de la bonté, et aussi une justesse d'esprit, une grande bonne foi, il ne parle guère de ce qu'il ne connaît pas; il accepte ses limites. (29)

From afar Thérèse paints a favorable portrait of Bernard and spends the first part of the novel preparing her *apologia* in an effort to explain to him her failed attempt on his life. Upon seeing him again, however, she realizes immediately the futility of her effort: "Durant tout ce voyage, elle s'était efforcée, à son insu, de recréer un Bernard capable de la comprendre, d'essayer de la comprendre...." (80). Bernard gets very little praise in the novel, except from his own mother for whom "... il était un saint; toute la famille le louait de sa grandeur d'âme...." (83). In a similar way, and in spite of his republicanism which she abhors, Mme de la Trave says of M. Larroque: "Le père pense mal, c'est entendu; mais il ne lui [à Thérèse] a donné que de bons exemples; c'est un saint laïque" (32). Canonization is an easier process for her than for Rome. Yet it is Thérèse who paints for the reader the definitive portrait both of her father and of Bernard. Bernard is "le plus précis des hommes" (24) who belongs "à la race aveugle, à la race implacable des simples" (32), a sexual sadist with Thérèse, a brutalizer of women in his treatment of the forelorned Anne, and an anti-Semite for whom "tous les Juifs se valent" (43).

For the briefest moment at the very end of the novel when he asks why she had tried to kill him, Bernard does, in fact, become for Thérèse "un homme nouveau," for "[e]lle avait, à son insu, troublé Bernard" (110). Yet, because Thérèse cannot, even now, after all her introspection, clearly explain her act except to say finally "je cédais à un affreux devoir" (112), she realizes that this new Bernard, "une seconde rapproché, s'était de nouveau éloigné à l'infini" (112).

If, for the reader, the unintended but high irony of Mme de la Trave's use of "saint" in her descriptions of both her son and her brother-in-law is palpable, Mauriac is much less ready to canonize his eponymous heroine whom he admits he would like to see, according to his prefatory remarks, as a Saint Locuste, a repentant poisoner. Yet the author refrains from allowing a conversion for fear of his pious readers' putative revulsion at such an utterly implausible turn.

The curate and Jean Azévédo are the only secondary characters whom Mauriac draws as, in any way, sympathetic. The curate is the more unknown; he is even nameless. And like Thérèse's and like Azévédo's, his behavior draws down the condemnation of the family:

> Il est très exact, disait Madame de la Trave; il fait son adoration tous les soirs; mais il manque d'onction, je ne le trouve pas ce qui s'appelle pieux. Et pour les oeuvres, il laisse tout tomber.... C'est très joli d'avoir toujours le nez dans ses livres, mais une paroisse est vite perdue. (70)

For Thérèse, it is the curate's solitary life which intrigues her and which makes her see him as so much like her, for he leads, like her, an apparently desolate existence. While his Sunday sermons fail to offer her any insight into his personality, she clearly imagines him as someone, in some ways, very like herself:

Ah! lui, peut-être, aurait-il pu l'aider à débrouiller en elle ce monde confus.... (70)

Later when thinking of her own solitude and the mistaken hope of ever finding others like herself, Thérèse chooses an image to describe her own isolation which is much more repugnant than the image of the desert created around the curate by the cassock he wears:

> Dire qu'elle a cru qu'il existait un endroit du monde où elle aurait pu s'épanouir au milieu d'êtres qui l'eussent comprise, peut-être admirée, aimée! Mais sa solitude lui est attachée plus étroitement qu'au lépreux son ulcère.... (79)

Jean Azévédo, another outsider, a sickly Jew, who has come to his family's country home in nearby Vilméja for his health, exerts the greater influence on Thérèse, and much of the content of their conversations is reported in the novel. André Joubert suggests that this character was inspired by Gide, and clearly some of what Azévédo preaches has the ring of the Nietzschean, self-realization imperative of *L'Immoraliste*.[7]

Azévédo's most perceptive and undeniably accurate comments concern the nature of the provincial society which Thérèse inhabits. He uses two images drawn from the topography of the surrounding region to describe the inhabitants' lives: "Regardez, me disait-il, cette immense et uniforme surface de gel où toutes les âmes ici sont prises.... Il faut se soumettre à ce morne destin commun ...." (63). Those who resist, he surmises, disappear: "... parfois une crevasse découvre l'eau noire: quelqu'un s'est débattu, a disparu; la croûte se reforme" (63). Thérèse agrees and confirms the uncanny accuracy of his observation. Likewise, he tells Thérèse, and she comes to believe, that her very thoughts are limited and constrained by the thoughts of those around her:

> De même qu'ici toutes les voitures sont "à la voie", c'est-à-dire assez larges pour que les roues correspondent exactement aux ornières des charrettes, toutes mes pensées jusqu'à ce jour, avaient été "à la voie" de mon père, de mes beaux parents. (60)

For Thérèse, secularly trained at her lycée and intellectually curious, and a reader unlike Anne or any of the family, Azévédo represents a kindred spirit. For her, "il était le premier homme que je rencontrais et pour qui comptait plus que tout la vie de l'esprit" (60). For Azévédo, the important rule in life is "devenir soi-même" (63). "Et encore: 'S'accepter,' cela oblige les meilleurs d'entre nous à s'affronter eux-mêmes, mais à visage découvert et dans un combat sans ruse" (64).

Despite the perspicacity of Azévédo's observations and the appeal of his philosophy and its aptness for Thérèse's life, the reader is warned from the moment Thérèse recalls her first conversation with Azévédo that his influence on her was perhaps less significant than she had at first imagined. While specifically about the question of religion, a perennial topic in this family divided between anti-clerical, republican Larroques and conservative, Catholic Desqueyroux, Jean's ideas, which at first had greatly impressed Thérèse, prove, upon reflection, to have been of little real value: "Je crois bien que je vomirais aujourd'hui ce ragoût...." (59). Further evidence of the minor import of Azévédo and his philosophy on Thérèse comes, if needed, from Mauriac himself who, as noted, execrates self-satisfaction. Thérèse at one point thinks of those beings "qui ne souhaitent que connaître, que comprendre,—selon un mot qu'avait répété Jean *avec un air de satisfaction profonde* 'devenir ce qu'ils sont'" (62, my emphasis). At the end of the novel too, when she gets up from lunch to begin her life in Paris, Thérèse decides not to go see Azévédo because

> Elle connaissait Jean Azévédo; mais les êtres dont elle souhaitait l'approche, elle ne les connaissait pas; elle savait d'eux seulement qu'ils n'exigeraient guère de paroles. (115)[8]

And so similarly, one may conclude, Azévédo's rule about self-actualization and self-acceptance which had initially impressed Thérèse proves less than useful in the long run to this woman torn between traditional family and personal fulfillment. At the end of the novel, in her final conversation with Bernard, Thérèse realizes that she simply cannot jettison either part of her dual personality.

The utterly irresolvable dilemma of Thérèse, of the two Thérèses, becomes transparently evident here as Thérèse herself finally realizes and tries to articulate her dual nature. Jacques Petit glosses this passage (113) by identifying Anne as a representative of one of the poles toward which Thérèse tends:

> En découvrant ainsi sa double nature, Thérèse éclaire le personnage d'Anne de la Trave qui joue dans le roman le rôle qui aurait pu être le sien: celui d'une femme qui accepte son rôle familial et social, se résigne à l'effacement. Elle fait mieux sentir aussi le sens de son drame: elle se révolte, mais elle est au fond incapable de se libérer de son milieu; elle en a les idées, les goûts et jusqu'aux préventions.[9]

The Larroque-Desqueyroux-la Trave clan all share the same values, while Thérèse, by her own admission, both yearns for the security of family, and yet seeks the intellectual élan of Azévédo and the quiet independence and apparent peace of the curate resigned to his difference and to his consequent solitude. Both of these outsiders—the philosopher and the cleric—can lead their lives following their personal ethic, respectively, of rigorous self-fulfillment and consecration to an ordered, contemplative life. Yet, unlike the curate's, Thérèse's solitude has no transcendent underpinnings. In marrying, Thérèse "s'incrustait dans un bloc familial, 'elle se casait'; elle entrait dans un ordre" (33).[10] The too strict observance required by this familial order leads to Thérèse's expulsion for it. Just as Justin and Madame Homais are Charles and Emma in another key, so too all the characters in *Thérèse Desqueyroux*, both the family and the outsiders, embody values Thérèse yearns for, yet so diametrically opposed are these values that she is unable to embrace all of them successfully at the same time. She is doomed to be unhappy, whether sequestered at Argelouse or free in Paris. Each place, representing each sort of yearned-for life, attracts her to its orbit with a powerful pull. The thoughts Thérèse has as she begins her new life in Paris are intertwined with recollections of the life of the other Thérèse at Argelouse:

> Thérèse ne redoutait plus la solitude. Il suffisait qu'elle demeurât immobile: comme son corps, étendu dans la lande du Midi, eût attiré les fourmis, les chiens, ici elle pressentait déjà autour de sa chair, une agitation obscure, un remous. (115)

What clearly is lacking in the experience of Thérèse is any role model able to suggest a life like the one she seeks. And little wonder! Her family is narrow and stifling and in it she fears the fate of her mother, dying in childbirth; fears becoming her own Aunt Clara; fears being excised from the family like her grand-mother Julie Bellade (whom, given Thérèse's fate at novel's end, she most resembles). There is little doubt that, like Julie Bellade's, Thérèse's photos too will be excised from the family's albums. The reader then can find little solace or much hope for this troubled woman who in the novel's stark conclusion begins her new life in Paris, not with any gusto or much enthusiasm at all, but by walking aimlessly along the street after a solitary lunch.

NOTES

1. See, for example, D. A. Williams, "The Role of Binet in *Madame Bovary*," *Romanic Review* 71 (1980): 149-166 and Mary Donaldson-Evans, "A Pox on Love: Diagnosing *Madame Bovary*'s Blind Beggar," *Symposium* 44, no. 1 (1990): 15-27. K. E. Curry and L. R. Andrews in "Emma Bovary's Lost Brother: A Study of Flaubert's Use of 'Minor' Details in the Structure of *Madame Bovary*," *Nineteenth-Century French Studies* 25, nos 1 & 2 (1996-1997): 92-99, contend that Emma spends her life searching for replacements for this dead "brother/lover" and suggest a whole series of fraternal substitutes, including Emma's yearned-for son who turns out in the end to be a daughter, Léon, Hippolyte, even Charles (after the operation on Hippolyte's club-foot and before the am-

putation), and Justin. See Appendix B for my response to Alan Raitt's "The Strange Case of Emma Bovary's Brother," *French Studies Bulletin* 66 (Spring 1998): 4-7.
    2. Gustave Flaubert, *Correspondance*, in *Oeuvres complètes* (Paris, Conard, 1927), 3: 291.
    3. Mauriac has stated categorically his hatred of the self-satisfied. In *Le Romancier et ses personnages* (see *Oeuvres romanesques et théâtrales complètes*, ed. Jacques Petit (Paris: Gallimard, 1979), 2: 852) he writes: "Le héros du *Noeud de Vipères* ou l'empoisonneuse Thérèse Desqueyroux, aussi horribles qu'ils apparaissent, sont dépourvus de la seule chose que je haïsse au monde et que j'ai peine à supporter dans une créature humaine, et qui est la complaisance et la satisfaction. Ils ne sont pas contents d'eux-mêmes, ils connaissent leur misère."
    4. The translator, who presumes heterosexuality to be the norm, has added as the last words "by a man" which are not in the French original.
    5. William Kidd, "Oedipal and pre-Oedipal Elements in *Thérèse Desqueyroux*," 25-46, in *François Mauriac: Visions and Reappraisals*, ed. John E. Flower and Bernard C. Swift, (Berg: Oxford, New York, Munich, 1989), 43, argues that Clara's death is a "symbolic re-enactment of the mother's death...."
    6. The question of what motivates Thérèse, not only to marry but later to attempt to kill Bernard, is a thorny one, with some critics faulting Mauriac as they decry her motives as unclear and emanating, therefore, from a flawed fictional creation. Into this group falls Tony Hunt in "Fatality and the Novel: *Tristram, Manon Lescaut* and *Thérèse Desqueyroux*," *Durham University Journal*, n. s. 37, no. 2 (1976): 183-195. Others see the uncertainty of her motivations as an integral part of her personality. See, for example, William Kidd (especially p. 26) and Jean Lacouture, *François Mauriac* (Paris: Seuil, 1980), 216.
    7. In his *François Mauriac et Thérèse Desqueyroux*, (Paris: Nizet, 1982), 90, André J. Joubert speaks of "cette morale naïvement gidienne d'Azévédo."
    8. For a study of Mauriac's sexually evocative use of the word "*être*" in the novel, see the second section of Chapter 2 above.
    9. *Oeuvres romanesques et théâtrales complètes*, ed. Jacques Petit, 2: 991, note 1.
    10. Jacques Petit (*Oeuvres romanesques et théâtrales complètes*, 2: 921) makes the astute observation that "Anne devient une sorte de 'double' qui à tout instant incarne, dans le mouvement romanesque, la contradiction profonde de Thérèse...." One might perhaps more precisely call Anne an "inverted double," for as Petit himself says "elle se révolte, en s'éprenant de Jean Azévédo, au moment où Thérèse 'se case', tente de 'se sauver' en se mariant, et lorsque la jeune fille se soumet à son tour, c'est Thérèse qui se révolte." By applying René Girard's theories to the novel, Timothy Williams in "Thérèse and Anne: Mauriac's Mimetic Rivals," *Romance Quarterly* 48, no. 2 (2001): 75-88, makes a convincing case for seeing the two women as inextricably bound, with Thérèse modeling her behavior on Anne's and, when frustrated in so doing, acting as an obstacle to Anne's realizing her desires. Williams states that his reading "is an important key to explaining the violence of the novel's protagonist, one of Mauriac's most enigmatic characters" (76). While he does quite nicely suggest a plausible explanation for some of Thérèse's behavior, his univocal reading, in the end, closes down rather than opening up the enigma that is Thérèse. Despite his contention that his reading is an "important key" for explaining Thérèse's violence, Williams at no time explains or even discusses why Thérèse poisoned Bernard!

CHAPTER VI

Photo Negativity in *Madame Bovary* and *Thérèse Desqueyroux*

In *Madame Bovary*, the burgeoning state of the recently invented art of photography is suggested by a single reference to a daguerreotype. Charles asks Léon to inquire about the cost of one of himself which Charles wants to present to Emma. In this way, Flaubert underscores, and not for the first time, the husband's blindness to his wife's indifference to, indeed, her utter scorn for him as he, quite unaware, contemplates buying her such an astonishingly inappropriate gift:

> ... [Charles] le pria de voir lui-même à Rouen quels pouvaient être les prix d'un beau daguerréotype; c'était une surprise sentimentale qu'il réservait à sa femme, une attention fine, son portrait en habit noir. (163)[1]

The few other references to artistic renderings of characters in Flaubert's novel also serve as reinforcements of negative feelings of disappointment, abandonment, or betrayal. No image serves as a cherished reminder of a loved one. Photographs will have much the same function a half-century later in *Thérèse Desqueyroux*. In these two modern novels, we are far from the secretive and almost fetishistic use of portraits by respectful lovers for whom the portrait, the virtual representation of the unattainable beloved, must suffice.

M. de Nemours purloins a miniature of the eponymous heroine of *la Princesse de Clèves* which belongs to her husband; Mme de Clèves, alone in her garden pavilion at Coulommiers, gazes at the image of Nemours who figures in a canvas depicting the siege of Metz.[2]

In *Madame Bovary*, too, miniatures of the lovers, Emma and Rodolphe, play an important, yet different, role. Rodolphe comes across a miniature of

Emma in his box of amorous mementos as he prepares to write her, breaking off their liaison and planned flight to Italy:

> Il y avait auprès, se cognant à tous les angles, la miniature donnée par Emma; sa toilette lui parut prétentieuse et son regard *en coulisse* du plus pitoyable effet.... (266)

This gratuitous denigration of her image precedes his comparison of her portrait and his memory of her, all of which ends remarkably in his total erasure of Emma from his mind, despite his holding her very image before his eyes:

> ... à force de considérer cette image et d'évoquer le souvenir du modèle, les traits d'Emma peu à peu se confondirent en sa mémoire, comme si la figure vivante et la figure peinte, se frottant l'une contre l'autre, se fussent réciproquement effacées. (266-267)

Rodolphe stands here in stark contrast to Charles who ironically, after Emma's death, cannot recapture her image in his mind despite all his efforts:

> Une chose étrange, c'est que Bovary, tout en pensant à Emma continuellement, l'oubliait; et il se désespérait à sentir cette image lui échapper de la mémoire au milieu des efforts qu'il faisait pour la retenir. (441)

Toward the end of the novel, upon finding the letter Rodolphe had sent Emma rejecting the idea of fleeing to Italy and breaking off their affair, Charles decides that any affection the writer might have had for Emma must have been simply platonic. Later though, Charles finds all the correspondence Emma had kept both from Léon and from Rodolphe, as well as a portrait of Rodolphe. It is the portrait of this other man which plunges Charles into utter despair and almost total isolation:

> Il découvrit une boîte, la défonça d'un coup de pied. Le portrait de Rodolphe lui sauta en plein visage, au milieu des billets doux bouleversés.
> On s'étonna de son découragement. Il ne sortait plus, ne recevait personne, refusait même d'aller voir ses malades. (443-444)

Soon afterwards, Rodolphe himself sits across from a Charles now aware of the truth. Bovary's first thought is how much he would have liked to be this man so loved by Emma. At the conclusion of their strained encounter, Charles proffers a high minded, but totally erroneous, explanation of all that has happened. He blames not Rodolphe whose image and letters Emma cherished despite Rodolphe's rejection of her, but rather fate.

In *Thérèse Desqueyroux*, no actual photos of Thérèse figure into the story. Photographs of others, however, serve various ends: as a focus for the bourgeois virtue of conformity; for the heroine's jealousy; for the stunted emotional development of her husband; and for the cruel consequences of Thérèse's sequestration at Argelouse on the eponymous heroine herself and its effect on Bernard too.

In the novel's very first scene, as Thérèse leaves the courthouse with her lawyer and her father, she conjures up what Mauriac describes tellingly as the "visage inconnu" of her grandmother:

> [Thérèse] aspira de nouveau la nuit pluvieuse, comme un être menacé d'étouffement; et soudain s'éveilla en elle le visage inconnu de Julie Bellade, sa grand'mère maternelle—inconnu: on eût cherché vainement chez les Larroque ou chez les Desqueyroux un portrait, un daguerréotype, une photographie de cette femme dont nul ne savait rien, sinon qu'elle était partie un jour. Thérèse imagine qu'*elle aurait pu être ainsi effacée, anéantie*, et plus tard il n'eût même pas été permis à sa fille, à sa petite Marie, de retrouver dans un album la figure de celle qui l'a mise au monde. (17, my emphasis)

The phrase "elle aurait pu être ainsi effacée, anéantie" of the last sentence will prove especially ironic as Thérèse returns to her husband and family where she becomes the victim of their cruelty and, eventually, it is apparent, among whom she is sure to become yet another "inconnue" like the absent Julie Bellade of the novel's opening chapter.

While talking with Jean Azévédo, who decries provincial conformity by describing this rural society of les Landes as "cette immense et uniforme surface de gel où toutes les âmes ici sont prises" (63), Thérèse again alludes not to Julie Bellade specifically, but to still others in her family who apparently suffered the very same fate. Their photos too have been removed:

> Parfois je me suis enquis de tel grand-oncle, de telle aïeule, dont les photographies ont disparu de tous les albums, et je n'ai jamais recueilli de réponse sauf, une fois, cet aveu: "Il a disparu ... on l'a fait disparaître." (63)

After Thérèse's return to Argelouse, the second panel of a grand-motherly diptych appears and contrasts with the now-empty first panel once occupied by Julie Bellade. Thérèse's missing and disowned maternal grandmother is present to Thérèse only as a constant absence, recalled solely by blank spaces in the family photo album. Other photos remain at the Desqueyroux house at Argelouse. Along with the discolored outlines marking the walls where some photos recently taken to Saint-Clair once hung, three photos remain:

> Aux murs, la trace demeurait encore des portraits anciens qu'avait pris Bernard pour en orner le salon de Saint-Clair, —et les clous rouillés qui ne soutenaient plus rien. Sur la cheminée, dans un triple cadre de fausse écaille, des photographies étaient pâles comme si les

> morts qu'elles représentaient y fussent morts une seconde fois: le père de Bernard, sa grand'mère, Bernard lui-même coiffé "en enfant d'Edouard." (93-94)

It is here in this house, dominated by these ghostly figures of bourgeois rectitude: Bernard's dead father and Bernard's paternal grandmother, that Thérèse will remain sequestered. Bernard himself is also present here to Thérèse but significantly, he appears in a childhood photo. His appearance "coiffé en enfant d'Edouard," is further described in MS 2 of the novel as "avec une (robe) ridicule et une fleur dans la main droite"[3]

And so subsequently, it is this child-like and rather silly-looking Bernard who reacts with sympathy upon his return to Argelouse where he finds a Thérèse, now gaunt and emaciated after weeks of ill-nourishment and confinement to her bedroom. His concern, however, is not aroused by the pitiable state of his wife. Rather, while looking at her, what he sees in his imagination is a hauntingly unforgettable image from his youth:

> En une seconde, il revit cette image coloriée du *Petit Parisien*, qui parmi beaucoup d'autres, ornait les cabinets en planches du jardin d'Argelouse; —et tandis que bourdonnaient les mouches, qu'au dehors grinçaient les cigales d'un jour de feu, ses yeux d'enfant scrutaient ce dessin rouge et vert qui représentait la *Séquestrée de Poitiers*.
> Ainsi contemplait-il, maintenant, Thérèse, exsangue, décharnée .... (103)

His concern and fearful look have nothing at all to do, then, with Thérèse herself. At this moment, each of the spouses is in fact displaced. The child-Bernard sees again the image of the celebrated victim of her Poitevin family. Mauriac substitutes for the ill-matched couple "Bernard-Thérèse" other characters whose presence is evoked through the medium of pictures: the child-Bernard and *la Séquestrée de Poitiers*.[4] The reader has been made aware from his earlier mistreatment of his half-sister Anne de la Trave that Bernard is incapable of compassion for those who commit infractions against the family's law of utter conformity. To allow for a solution to Thérèse's sequestration without violating this bedrock trait of Bernard Desqueyroux's personality, Mauriac replaces Thérèse with an unrelated victim from a notorious *fait divers* which had moved a more empathetic, youthful Bernard. The child-Bernard had recoiled at the newspaper picture of the wretched woman imprisoned by her family. He now recoils again, apparently because of Thérèse's ghastly appearance but, in fact, because of his recall of a childhood trauma. Unaware of the substitution Bernard has made—whereby Thérèse is no longer seen as Thérèse but as *la Séquestrée de Poitiers*—Thérèse herself cannot fathom Bernard's unexpected reaction to "her:"

Thérèse l'observe, assis en face d'elle et tisonnant, mais ne devine
pas l'image que contemplent ses gros yeux dans la flamme; ce dessin
rouge et vert du *Petit Parisien*: *la Séquestrée de Poitiers*. (106)

An even most memorable scene in the novel involving the photo of one of the characters occurs in Bernard and Thérèse's Paris hotel room during the final stop on their wedding trip. Opening and reading, according to the order of the postmarks, three letters sent by Anne and only now arrived, having followed them from city to city on their itinerary, Thérèse learns of Anne's relationship with Jean Azévédo, the sickly Jewish intellectual recuperating at his family's nearby country house. It is in the third envelope that she finds his photo:

Près de la fenêtre, elle contempla ce visage: c'était un jeune garçon
dont la tête, à cause des cheveux épais, semblait trop forte.... Jean
Azévédo se dressait, pareil à David.... Il portait sa veste sur les bras;
sa chemise était un peu ouverte ... "c'est ce qu'il appelle la dernière
caresse permise...." (40-41)

An already unhappily married Thérèse reacts angrily to this proof of Anne's apparent amorous delight: "Elle connaît cette joie ... et moi, alors? et moi? pourquoi pas moi?" (41). And now as Thérèse recalls all this, she recalls too what she did at the end of the scene in the hotel:

Il y a deux ans déjà, dans cette chambre d'hôtel, j'ai pris l'épingle,
j'ai percé la photographie de ce garçon à l'endroit du coeur, —non
pas furieusement, mais avec calme et comme s'il s'agissait d'un acte
ordinaire; —aux lavabos, j'ai jeté la photographie ainsi transpercée;
j'ai tiré la chasse d'eau. (41)

After a dinner in the Bois de Boulogne marked by Thérèse's volley of attacks against her family and Bernard's, calling them new-comers compared to the Azévédos and, like the Azévédos, no more exempt than these Portuguese Jews from sickness and genetic flaws, Thérèse, having virtually "disposed of" Azévédo earlier in the day, thinks of getting rid of Bernard now lying beside her in bed:

D'une main brutale et qui pourtant ne l'éveilla pas, de nouveau elle
l'écarta.... Ah! l'écarter une fois pour toute et à jamais! le précipiter
hors du lit, dans les ténèbres. (44)

Already on her honeymoon, the stage seems set for Thérèse's later attempt on Bernard's life. She wants to destroy the cause of Anne's happiness; she wants to be free of the cause of her own unhappiness. When Thérèse finally meets Azévédo, she learns he is not at all seriously interested in Anne. Azévédo's ethic of individual self-fulfillment, in fact, intensifies for Thérèse the sense of repression she feels in the Desqueyroux family. She had not really needed to get rid of

Azévédo; Bernard, however, is another story. Capable of calm murderous feelings in her ritualistic "murder" of Azevedo, Thérèse will soon describe her slow, deliberate, and relentless campaign to poison Bernard, all of which will be yet another series of "actes ordinaires."

In Flaubert, images of the characters serve to undercut rather than to underscore the affection felt for the person represented virtually on canvas or paper. A daguerreotype of Charles could never be a gift welcomed by Emma, just as Thérèse hardly values the photo of Azévédo sent her by an ecstatically amorous Anne. Emma's pretentious face in the miniature is no longer recognizable to a Rodolphe intent on ending an affair gone awry, while Bernard looking directly at a haggard Thérèse can see only another wretched face from an old magazine article.

For Mauriac, photos serve to displace characters, to allow them to act in unexpected ways, to foreshadow possibilities. Bernard will free from home confinement, not Thérèse, but the woman whose image scarred his child's psyche: *la Séquestrée de Poitiers*. Thérèse is quite capable of murdering Bernard, for her rage at seeing Azévédo's photo firmly establishes the nature and intensity of her fury. In the end, Thérèse comes more and more to resemble her maternal grandmother. Unlike the "good" grandmother, Bernard's paternal grandmother, whose spectral photo watches over the family still, Thérèse like her own maternal grandmother, Julie Bellade, will be excised from the family's albums and so from their memory. For her own daughter Marie, Thérèse will be yet another familial "visage inconnu."[5]

NOTES

1. Adrianne Tooke in her extraordinarily rich study *Flaubert and the Pictorial Arts: From Image to Text* (Oxford: Oxford U. P., 2000), 56-58, discusses Flaubert's own disdain for the art of photography when he writes this reply on 14 August 1853 to Louise Colet who had offered him a picture of herself: "... ne m'envoie pas ton portrait photographié. Je déteste les photographies à proportion que j'aime les originaux. Jamais je ne trouve cela *vrai*." Tooke in her footnote to this passage mentions Charles's intended gift.

2. Madame de Lafayette, *la Princesse de Clèves* (Paris: Garnier-Flammarion, 1996). For Nemours' theft of her portrait, see pp. 136-137; concerning Mme de Clèves and the picture of Nemours, see p. 205.

3. François Mauriac, *Oeuvres romanesques et théâtrales complètes*, ed. Jacques Petit, (Paris: Gallimard, 1979), 2: 985.

4. For a study of this criminal case from 1901 which Mauriac refers to in the novel, see Jean-Marie Augustin, *L'histoire véridique de la Séquestrée de Poitiers*, (Paris:

Fayard, 2001). The following web-site also offers texts and images about the case: <http://sequestreedepoitiers.free.fr>

5. Of course, in subsequent stories Mauriac reunites Thérèse and Marie who become rivals for a young man's affection, for example, in the novel *La Fin de la nuit* (1935). I have not considered these sequels by Mauriac—two short stories and the aforementioned novel—for they are all much lesser literary works, by far, than *Thérèse Desqueyroux* and not germane to the Flaubert-Mauriac connection studied here.

Appendix A

A Response to Mary Orr's "Reflections on 'Bovarysme:' The Bovarys at Vaubyessard"

In her study of the novel's ball scene, Mary Orr highlights yet more of the myriad, significant Flaubertian details and reveals to us other, heretofore overlooked, facets of the network of interconnected references which echo profusely throughout *Madame Bovary*.[1] By uncovering for us the disguised milk and cherries whose exotic packaging as *une glace au marasquin* (83) so enchants Emma that she fails to recognize them as part of the familiar fabric of her own country-bourgeois existence, Mary Orr in an astute reading from the first part of the novel brings to this reader's mind an almost identical passage in Part III, Chapter 3, but one where such a disguise is lacking and, indeed, unnecessary.

During Emma's idyll with Léon, these "deux Robinsons" dine at a restaurant on an island in the Rouen harbor where "Ils mangeaient de la friture d'éperlans, de la crème et des cerises" (335-336). Here in the final part of the novel, Emma no longer needs to engage in "over valorizing difference," but rather, having frequently exercised her powers of "bovarysme," she is now capable herself of romanticizing, embellishing, and transforming the quotidian, for she has had much practice. To cite just a few examples: after returning from the ball, she fires her maid and goes about molding her newly-hired, country-bred servant into a lady's maid (92); her affair with the calculating and Don Juanesque Rodolphe becomes for Emma a liaison between a courtesan and a prince (250), a concubine and a king (254); and the simple act of receiving communion is transformed in her mind into a mystical apotheosis of union with the divine (282).

For such a woman, fried fish followed by cherries and cream is rather mundane fare and hardly very special. Like all the natural beauty that she and Léon see around them during their outing, it is not likely a first either, but "ils n'avaient sans doute jamais admiré tout cela, comme si la nature n'existait pas auparavant, ou qu'elle n'eût commencé à être belle que depuis l'assouvissement de leurs désirs" (336).

NOTE

1. Mary Orr, "Reflections on 'Bovarysme:' the Bovarys at Vaubyessard," *French Studies Bulletin* 61 (Winter 1996): 6-8.

Appendix B

A Response to Alan Raitt's "The Strange Case of Emma Bovary's Brother" and More

Critics have not failed to mention the isolated references in *Madame Bovary* to Emma's brother, both made by M. Rouault. After Emma's marriage, her father drives the newly-weds as far as Vassonville and, while returning to les Bertaux, he recalls the early days of his own married life and thinks "Comme c'était vieux tout cela! Leur fils, à présent, aurait trente ans" (56). Much later, talking with Charles after Emma's funeral, M. Rouault laments "Ah! c'est la fin pour moi, voyez-vous! J'ai vu partir ma femme ..., mon fils après ..., et voilà ma fille, aujourd'hui" (434). The chronological order of the deaths which he lists could not be clearer: Emma's mother, Emma's brother, and now Emma herself.

In his recent study, Alan Raitt argues that we have a real puzzle on our hands if indeed Emma's brother died after Emma's mother; that is, after Emma's return to les Bertaux from her convent-school.[1] And so to put the puzzle back on the shelf, Raitt contends that Flaubert made a mistake, and argues against the possibility of the brother's death as an adult this way: "... had his death been so recent, the father would hardly have reflected that the son would now have been thirty years old" (5). Now, is that conclusion quite so self-evident as Raitt suggests? On such occasions as the birthday of a deceased relative or at family funerals, one might well say (and I have found myself saying): "Mother would be eighty this year." One might not remember every year (but one certainly could), but certainly for those anniversaries marking a decade's turning, a recollection like M. Rouault's (*pace* Raitt) seems really quite natural, even a recollection two or three years later of a son dead in his late twenties.

Let's take Flaubert at his word: Emma's brother, to whom *she* never clearly refers, died relatively recently and, therefore, in his late twenties; that is to say, according to the text, after the death of her mother, another "strange case" of a family member Emma refers to but once after leaving school in Rouen to take her mother's place at les Bertaux. Speaking about both their deceased mothers, Emma says to Rodolphe that she is sure "... là-haut, ensemble, elles approuvent notre amour" (229).

Some speculations about Emma's dead brother—where he dies, presicely when, and how—remain utterly futile. Somewhat less audacious perhaps is the suggestion I will offer here that Emma may well be referring to her dead brother and describing his life as she thinks about her soon-to-be born child: "Elle souhaitait un fils; il serait fort et brun, elle l'appellerait Georges.... Un homme, au moins, est libre; il peut parcourir les passions et les pays, traverser les obstacles, mordre aux bonheurs les plus lointains" (128).

More audacious perhaps is this hypothesis. We may well know still more about Emma's mysterious brother. Emma's brother may have married. At the end of *Madame Bovary*, Berthe, the orphaned daughter of Emma and Charles, is sent to live first with her paternal grandmother. Madame Bovary *mère* dies within the year, becoming the third woman so named to die in the course of the novel. Emma's father, *le père* Rouault, cannot care for Berthe because he has become paralyzed in the time since his daughter's suicide. And so, for the hapless Berthe "ce fut une tante qui s'en chargea. Elle est pauvre et l'envoie, pour gagner sa vie, dans une filature de coton" (446). This passage contains the only use of the word "tante" in the novel and the only reference to yet another member of the Rouault or the Bovary family.

Who is this aunt? The OED gives as one of the definitions of hypothesis: "a supposition or conjecture put forth to account for known facts." How might we account then for the known fact of this aunt's existence?

Charles had no siblings. The two scant, yet tantalizing, references to Emma's dead brother say nothing about his having a wife. Yet the widowed wife of Emma's brother seems to be the most probable aunt to whom Berthe can have been sent; unless, of course, as seems highly unlikely, she was sent to a sister of *la veuve* Dubuc, Charles's first wife, or to a spouse of a dead Dubuc brother. Now, if the aunt was in fact a great aunt, that is a sibling or a sister-in-law of le *père* Rouault or of Madame Bovary *mère*, Flaubert could have used the *mot juste*, the perfectly good French word "grand-tante."

While *Le Grand Robert* does indicate under the entry "tante" that "On emploie aussi *tante* pour *grand-tante*,"[2] if one searches through other nineteenth-century novels, one finds both words used. In *Les Misérables*, for example, there are 57 instances of *tante*, three of *grand-tante*; in *Le Rouge et le Noir, tante* appears 10 times, *grand-tante* once; in *Le Père Goriot, tante* 16 times, *grand-tante* once.[3] It is true though that in *Goriot* both words, *tante* and *grand-tante*, are used to refer to Rastignac's aunt.

Flaubert writes that "ce fut *une* tante" rather than "*sa* tante." Was there then more than one aunt available? Here Balzac may be of more help. In *Le Père Goriot*, Balzac uses the indefinite article when he first introduces Rastignac's aunt, Madame de Marcillac: "Son père, sa mère, ses deux frères, ses deux soeurs, et une tante dont la fortune consistait en pensions, vivaient sur la petite terre de Rastignac" (49). In 13 of the 15 subsequent uses of *tante* in the novel—except for "le style de tante" and "la tante"—the term is invariably modified by the possessives *ma* or *ta* or *sa*. Flaubert's usage, when he writes in his first and only mention of Berthe's final guardian that "ce fut *une* tante," seems to follow not only Balzac's but common usage as well. In referring to an orphaned child raised by a member of the family other than her own parents, one might well say to someone unfamiliar with the family, "She was raised by an aunt." And that, even when there is only one aunt in the family.

So what does it matter if, in fact, Berthe must earn her keep in the house of Emma's dead brother's widow? It might well suggest that both Emma and her ne'er-do-well brother, both dead in their twenties, lived such self-centered lives that they left devastation in their wakes. Emma's infidelities prove fatal to Charles and her profligacy proves economically ruinous to Berthe. Is it possible that Emma's brother's fatal adventures left his widow penniless? These two female survivors, Berthe and her aunt, bear the family name, and will be the last to do so, for at the death of whichever survives the other, the name Bovary will die out.

In his final footnote, Alan Raitt dismisses out-of-hand the "interesting and controversial" article by Kristina E. Curry and Larry R. Andrews entitled "Emma Bovary's Lost Brother: A Study of Flaubert's Use of 'Minor' Details in the Structure of *Madame Bovary*," simply by labelling as "inherently self-contradictory" the novel's two passages on the brother, passages on which these authors base their argument that Emma seeks a replacement for her dead "brother/lover."[4] In the last sentence of his article, Raitt calls for an academic Chief Inspector Morse to solve the mystery of Emma's brother. I make no claim to such an exalted role. Perhaps the highest calling to which I can aspire is a markèdly lesser one of an academic Detective Sergeant Lewis or, lesser still, of a Chief Superintendent Strange. "First, a brother for Emma; now, an aunt for Berthe! What *are* we to make of all this?"

NOTES

1. Alan Raitt, "The Strange Case of Emma Bovary's Brother," *French Studies Bulletin* 66 (Spring 1998): 4-7.
2. *Le Grand Robert de la Langue Française*. (Paris: Dictionnaires Le Robert, 2001), 6:1007.

3. Searchable texts of 100 French classics are available from Biblionet through PhiloLogic at the University of Chicago's ARTFL site at the following address: <http://humanities.uchicago.edu/orgs/ARTFL/>
4. *Nineteenth-Century French Studies* 25, nos. 1 & 2 (1996-1997): 92-99.

Appendix C

Heavenly Bodies: Dogmatic Parody in Flaubert's *Un Coeur Simple*

Murray Sachs once summed up the results of one hundred years of critical readings of Flaubert's short story *Un coeur simple* (1877) in this way: "Critics still cannot agree ... whether *Un coeur simple* is a work of tender pity or bitter irony."[1]

While a detailed review of critical reaction to the tale would constitute a study in itself, suffice it to recall proponents of the polar positions which Sachs describes. Along with others including Enid Starkie and Jonathan Culler, Benjamin Bart takes Flaubert at his word concerning the nature of *Un coeur simple*. Bart, who recalls that Flaubert "wrote Gertrude Collier Tennant that it was a tender story," interprets the ending of Flaubert's tale in strict accordance with this authorial declaration.[2] Bart concludes concerning Flaubert's intentions that "to those who live lives of simple abnegation, his heart and his respect went out. He admired Félicité and asked his reader to join him in believing that those who are pure in heart will see God. Félicité did" (696). "Did, indeed!," one might exclaim. I shall return to this point later.

Ben Stoltzfus, with others, sees the tale replete rather with "hidden irony."[3] For him: "Beneath the detailed realism of Félicité's mysticism lurks Flaubert's attack on organized religion and the church" (20). Stoltzfus goes out of his way though to spare Félicité: "It is not an attack on Félicité. Félicité is merely the dupe of religious faith. It is the veiled attack on religion which gives the story its irony and its point of view" (20). His interpretation of the tale's ending is that "to have Loulou represent the spiritual comforts of faith is the supreme mockery" (22-23).

The tale ends with this sentence:

> Les mouvements de son coeur se ralentirent un à un, plus vagues
> chaque fois, plus doux, comme une fontaine s'épuise, comme un
> écho disparaît; et, quand elle exhala son dernier souffle, elle crut voir,
> dans les cieux entrouverts, un perroquet gigantesque, planant au-
> dessus de sa tête.[4]

While Stoltzfus's conclusion concerning the irony and mockery of the tale is to my mind undeniably correct, his claim that Faubert's is a "veiled" attack on religion and his statement at the end of his article that: "At no point in the story, however, does [Flaubert] openly deride [religion]," are certainly highly questionable.[5] It seems clear that the end of *Un coeur simple* contains, in fact, an unmistakable, but heretofore overlooked, parody of one of the most central of Roman Catholic doctrines.

Most of those who have written on *Un coeur simple* allude to the Corpus Christi procession and the attendant adoration of the Eucharist which take place in the courtyard below, and are intercut with, Félicité's deathbed scene and final vision. Yet, no one has satisfactorily explained the meaning, significance, and relationship of these two juxtaposed and intertwined events; namely, the Eucharistic procession and Félicité's vision of what Stoltzfus has called "the Holy Parrot."

It is surprising, for example, that an eminent critic in the field of Flaubert studies like Benjamin Bart fails to grasp the import of the Corpus Christi procession and its function in the text. He is, at the same time, curiously enough, one of the few critics who has overlooked the fundamental and, as I hope to establish, crucial distinction between Christ and the Holy Spirit. It is worth quoting at length Bart's confusion of these two persons of the Trinity:

> Félicité's real devotion was for the Christ of the New Testament. She wept on hearing of His Passion and found all the humble things of her daily life recurring in His story and sanctified by His presence. The effort to understand what His person was like she abandoned wholly, contenting herself with the basis in superstition which was open to her simplicity: it was perhaps He who flickered over the swamps at night in the will-o'-the wisp. She paid no attention to dogma whatsoever, for it was beyond her comprehension; she dozed quietly while the priest expounded it and wakened only in time to take Virginie home. (693)

Flaubert, in point of fact, wrote the following describing Félicité's simple, down-to-earth reaction to the catechism lessons she heard with Virginie as the child prepared for her First Communion:

> Les semailles, les moissons, les pressoirs, toutes ces choses familières dont parle l'Evangile, se trouvaient dans sa vie; le passage de Dieu les avait sanctifiées; *et elle aima plus tendrement les agneaux pour l'amour de l'Agneau, les colombes à cause du Saint Esprit.* Elle avait

peine à imaginer sa personne; car il n'était pas seulement oiseau, mais encore un feu, et d'autres fois un souffle. C'est peut-être sa lumière qui voltige la nuit au bord des marécages.... (60, emphasis added)

It is, at this point, the appearance of the Holy Spirit which Félicité cannot imagine with certainty, for "sa personne" in this passage surely can only mean "la personne du Saint-Esprit." Later on, though, she will resolve the problem of his identity when *colombe / oiseau / feu / souffle* of the passage just cited all give way to *perroquet*—or more precisely to *un des ancêtres de Loulou*—in the wonderfully logical, abbreviated syllogism in which Félicité concludes that the Holy Spirit could not have been a dove:

Le Père, pour s'annoncer, n'avait pu choisir une colombe, puisque ces bêtes-là n'ont pas de voix, mais plutôt un des ancêtres de Loulou. (82)[6]

Whereas Bart misread what seems obvious and is clearly stated in Flaubert's text, others have not, for generally critics have underscored correctly Félicité's growing fusion of Loulou with the Holy Spirit. None, however, has noted the recurrent references throughout the tale pairing Christ and the Holy Spirit which culminate in the final scene with the simultaneous Eucharistic adoration and the glorious transfiguration of Loulou, *cru Saint Esprit*.

Flaubert, no fewer than three times before this final scene associates the two related, but utterly distinct, Trinitarian persons: Christ and the Holy Spirit. First, much as Villon's illiterate mother had scrutinized similar church decorations some four centuries earlier, Félicité studies the stained glass windows of the parish church:[7]

Quand elle avait fait à la porte une génuflexion, elle s'avançait sous la haute nef entre la double ligne des chaises, ouvrait le banc de Mme Aubain, s'asseyait et promenait ses yeux autour d'elle.
Les garçons à droite, les filles à gauche, emplissaient les stalles du choeur; le curé se tenait debout près du lutrin; sur un vitrail de l'abside, *le Saint Esprit dominait la Vierge: un autre la montrait à genoux devant l'Enfant-Jesus*.... (60, emphasis added)

It should be noted that Flaubert reinforces the connection between Christ and the Holy Sprit (and, of course, Loulou) throughout the tale. One of Loulou's three utterances "Je vous salue, Marie," while the beginning of a common prayer, is, in fact, part of the angelic salutation to Mary at the Annunciation or Incarnation of Jesus; see Luke 1, 26-35. In verse 35, the angel Gabriel reveals to Mary the role of the Holy Spirit in the Incarnation, saying "... the Holy Spirit shall come upon thee and the power of the Most High shall overshadow thee: therefore also that holy thing which shall be born of thee shall be called the Son of God." The

just discussed stained glass window in which "le Saint Esprit dominait la Vierge" illustrates this scriptural verse.[8]
Next comes the already quoted passage showing the simplicity of Félicité's faith:

> ... elle aima plus tendrement les agneaux par amour de l'Agneau [= le Christ], les colombes à cause du Saint-Esprit. (60)

And then one reads her conclusive identification of the Holy Spirit as a parrot ("Le Père, pour s'annoncer...."), based on her down-to-earth exegesis of this passage from the Synoptic Gospels describing the Baptism of Christ:

> And Jesus, when he was baptized, went up straightway out of the water and, lo, the heavens were opened unto him, and he saw the Spirit of God descending like a dove, and lighting upon him. And lo a voice from heaven, saying, This is my beloved son, in whom I am well pleased.[9]

Only a parrot, and certainly not a dove, could speak as the voice from heaven.

These three passages and Félicité's observation associating and, indeed, juxtaposing Christ—l'Enfant-Jésus / l'Agneau / the baptized Christ—with the Holy Spirit are hardly accidental or insignificant details, but rather iterative reinforcements of the final scene's juxtaposition of these two Trinitarian figures.[10] In the final scene of the story on the altar below Félicité's window are both the Eucharistic Christ and Loulou, already deified by Félicité who for some time has prayed not before the "image d'Epinal" representing the Holy Spirit but turned rather towards the stuffed parrot:

> Loulou, caché, sous des roses, ne laissait voir que son front bleu, pareil à une plaque de lapis. Les fabriciens, les chantres, les enfants se rangèrent sur les trois côtés de la cour. Le prêtre gravit lentement les marches, et posa sur la dentelle son grand soleil d'or qui rayonnait. Tous s'agenouillèrent. Il se fit un grand silence. Et les encensoirs, allant à pleine volée, glissaient sur leurs chaînettes. (87)

It is the consecrated host—the Corpus Domini or Corpus Christi—exposed before the crowd for its adoration, during this feast celebrating the real presence of Christ in the Eucharist, that is contained in the monstrance or ostensorium described in the text as *son grand soleil d'or*. The Corpus Christi procession bears public witness to the ancient Roman Catholic doctrine of Eucharistic transubstantiation which, according to what the *Catholic Encyclopedia* calls Thomas Aquinas's incisive formulation, referring to the bread consecrated at the Mass and reserved for the adoration of the faithful, holds that the "whole substance of the bread is changed into the whole substance of Christ's body."[11]

At the end of *Un coeur simple* there are presented on the altar, then, not one, but two transubstantiated divinities. While for the Church something so ordinary as common bread has become, it is believed, the Body of Christ, the stuffed parrot also present on the altar has become, at least for Félicité, the Holy Spirit. By finally leveling these two entities, the Eucharistic Christ and the *perroquet gigantesque*, Flaubert perforce makes the latter a grotesque parody of the former. Flaubert once again, and for at least the fourth time in the short tale, associates Christ and the Holy Spirit, now conflated with Loulou, and suggests thereby that the Church's belief that bread is the Body of Christ is no more or less extraordinary or, for some, quaint or, for others, ridiculous, than Félicité's belief that the Holy Spirit is a gigantic transmogrified Loulou. As we saw in Chapter 3, Mauriac too uses *la Fête-Dieu,* the feast of Corpus Christi, to underscore Bernard's bourgeois conformity and hypocrisy and, especially, Thérèse's visceral, negative reaction to her husband's inauthentic behavior.

It is not only within the text of *Un coeur simple* itself that one finds confirmation of this parodic reading. The parodic nature of Emma's final vision of the blind beggar's "face hideuse" has already been discussed in Chapter 3 above. In addition, the parallel between Félicité's final vision and that of Saint Julien l'Hospitalier is also quite remarkable, for the unparodic ending of the latter serves to confirm and underscore the parodic nature of the former. At the conclusion of *Saint Julien l'Hospitalier*, the second of Flaubert's *Trois Contes*, the leper becomes a gigantic, transfigured Jesus Christ, just as in *Un coeur simple* Loulou is transformed into a gigantic "Holy Parrot." *Saint Julien l'Hospitalier* concludes with this description of the spectacular, apocalyptic transformation:

> Alors le lépreux l'étreignit; et ses yeux tout à coup prirent une clarté d'étoiles; ses cheveux s'allongèrent comme les rais du soleil; le souffle de ses narines avait la douceur des roses; un nuage d'encens s'éleva du foyer, les flots chantaient ... et celui dont les bras le [Julien] serraient toujours grandissait, grandissait, touchant de sa tête et de ses pieds les deux murs de la cabane. Le toit s'envola, le firmament se déployait; —et Julien monta vers les espaces bleus, face à face avec Notre-Seigneur Jésus, qui l'emportait dans le ciel. (130)

One cannot overlook either in the endings of each of these two tales the presence of at least three shared lexical elements, the presence of which underscores the relationship between these scenes. In each there are references to roses, the rays of the sun, and incense.

If parody, at its simplest, can be defined as exaggerated imitation designed to ridicule, the parody of the Catholic doctrine of transubstantiation in Félicité's final vision of the *perroquet gigantesque* during the Corpus Christi celebration seems to be strikingly obvious, not all gratuitous, nor even terribly ambiguous.[12] A critic like Stirling Haig, though, reads the end of the tale in a very different way. He concludes his article on *Un coeur simple* with a quote from *Bouvard et Pécuchet*, the writing of which Flaubert had interrupted in order to write the

Trois Contes. "Returning to his pair of idiots, he perhaps gave them," Haig suggests, "the definitive statement on belief; when Bouvard scoffs at the sight of their servant Marcel kneeling in prayer, Pécuchet's rejoinder is this: 'Qu'importe la croyance! Le principal est de croire.'"[13] Perhaps! Yet the coincidence in the text of *Un coeur simple* itself of a public profession of the Roman Catholic belief in Eucharistic transubstantiation and Félicité's belief in the divinity of her moth-eaten, stuffed parrot, works rather to the detriment and, indeed, the ridicule of the Church's belief.[14] Emma's vision of the hideous blindman's face subverts the anticipated Beatific Vision promised to those who, like Emma, receive the sacrament of Extreme Unction. Flaubert, describing Emma Bovary's death throes, recounts her anointing in the most tender way; yet as she expires, she sees a frightful sight and then ceases to exist. The presence in the final scene of *Un coeur simple* of this Eucharistic parody does not at all diminish the reader's sympathy for Féclicité, but rather constitutes yet another facet of a dénouement rich in meanings and evocations.[15]

In reading the end of *Un coeur simple*, as in reading the death scene from *Madame Bovary*, one is struck both by Flaubert's self-declared "*facultés de tendresse*" in his treatment of his heroines and, at the same time, by his capacity for trenchant and pitiless ridicule of religious dogma.

NOTES

1. Murray Sachs, "The Legacy of Flaubert," in *L'Hénaurme Siècle*, ed. Will L. McLendon (Heidelberg: C. Winter, 1984), 63.
2. Benjamin Bart, *Flaubert* (Syracuse: Syracuse U. P., 1967), 696. For the observations of Starkie and Culler, see Enid Starkie, *Flaubert the Master* (New York: Atheneum, 1971), 264, where she states: "There is no trace of irony in the story" and Jonathan Culler, *Flaubert: The Uses of Uncertainty* (Ithaca: Cornell U. P., 1974), 210, who states that "we can take the ending as finally transcending irony." Flaubert's epistolary comment, although Bart does not cite the source, must be his letter to Madame Tennant of 16 February 1877, see *Oeuvres complètes de Gustave Flaubert* (Paris, Club de l'Honnête Homme, 1975), 15: 540. Flaubert wrote: "Une question: pourquoi paraissez-vous étonnée de ce que j'aie pu faire un conte intitulé: *Un coeur simple*? Votre ébahissement m'intrigue. Douteriez-vous de mes facultés de tendresse? Vous n'avez pas ce devoir-là, vous!" For a succinct review of the various readings critics have given *Un coeur simple*, see Stirling Haig, "The Substance of Illusion in Flaubert's *Un coeur simple*," *Stanford French Review* 7 (1983): 301-02. Writing a decade later, Allan H. Pasco devotes a chapter (22-38) in his *Allusion: a Literary Graft* (Toronto: University of Toronto Press, 1994) to Flaubert's *Un coeur simple* and establishes himself firmly in the Bart / Culler /

Starkie camp, as he makes a case for seeing Félicité's life as a gloss on the Beatitudes of the New Testament.
3. Ben Stoltzfus, "Point of view in *Un coeur simple*," *French Review* 35 (1961): 19.
4. *Un coeur simple* in *Trois contes* (Paris, Petits Classiques Larousse, 1965), 87. Subsequent quotes from this story will be from this readily available edition.
5. Stoltzfus, 24.
6. Similarly François Villon's prayer-ballad which he writes for his untutored mother contains a wholly orthodox, but no less insightful, and startlingly simple, statement in which she identifies the Eucharist with the Incarnate Christ child: Vierge portant sans rompture encourir / Le sacrement qu'on célèbre à la messe. (vv. 890-91). See François Villon, *Complete Poems*, tr. Barbara N. Sargent-Baur (Toronto, Buffalo, London: University of Toronto Press, 1994), 114.
7. The poet's mother's conception of heaven and hell is very simple:
Au moustier voy dont suis paroissienne
Paradis paint ou sont harpes et lus
Et ung enfer ou dampnez sont boullus
L'ung me fait paour, l'autre joye et liesse. (vv. 895-898)
8. My former colleague and Flaubert scholar Anne Mullen Hohl, now at Seton Hall University, reminded me of the import of the angelic salutation to Mary.
9. Matthew 3, 16-17. See also Mark 1, 10-11 and Luke 3, 21-22.
10. Two other elements of the final sentence of the tale, it may be noted, are also foreshadowed earlier on. Recall that, in the end, Félicité "crut voir, *dans les cieux* entrouverts, un perroquet gigantesque *planant* au-dessus de sa tête." In the second section of the story, the reader learns that at the beginning of her service Félicité lived in Madame Aubain's house "dans une sorte de tremblement que lui causait 'le genre de la maison' et le souvenir de 'Monsieur' *planant* sur tout!" (52). Later, on the docks at Honfleur, where she goes to see Victor off, and where she becomes lost and confused: "... elle se crut folle, en apercevant *des chevaux dans le ciel*" (64, my emphasis). These animals which she sees in the sky above her are, the narrator then explains, raised up by pulleys and then lowered onto the ship for transport. Twenty years earlier in *Madame Bovary*, Flaubert had used a similar image to describe Emma's long-anticipated passion which, soon after her marriage, she erroneously thinks she actually possesses:
Mais l'anxiété d'un état nouveau, ou peut-être l'irritation causée par la présence de cet homme, avait suffi à lui faire croire qu'elle possédait enfin cette passion merveilleuse qui jusqu'alors s'était tenue *comme un grand oiseau au plumage rose planant dans la splendeur des ciels poétiques*: —et elle ne pouvait s'imaginer à présent que ce calme où elle vivait fût le bonheur qu'elle avait rêvé. (68, emphasis added).
11. *New Catholic Encyclopedia* (New York, 1967), 4: 259. For a brief study of the origins and the importance of the Feast of Corpus Christi, see Miri Rubin, "Corpus Christi: Inventing a Feast," *History* Today 40 (July 1990): 15-21.
12. On parody, see J. A. Cuddon, *A Dictionary of Literary Terms* (Garden City, N.Y.: Doubleday, 1977), 472-473 as well as the study by Joseph Dane, *Parody* (Norman and London: University of Oklahoma Press, 1988). Joseph G. Reish in an article entitled "Those who see God' in Flaubert's *Trois contes*," *Renascence* 34 (1984): 223, does not go at all far enough in explaining the final scene of the tale. He, like Culler, sees no parodic intent at all in this scene. Reish writes:

La Fête-Dieu or feast of Corpus Christi may have been chosen expressly by Flaubert for the day when Loulou becomes one with the Holy Spirit. On this feast day a significant "church sign" is given special recognition. The Body of Christ (Corpus Christi) is venerated under the form of the host which is carried in procession and displayed on repository altars. Félicité always looked forward in anticipation to this day and to her role in decorating the makeshift altars. The stuffed bird is her final contribution to the colorful display serving as a backdrop to the host, a sign of Christ. On this feast of a notable church sign, a personal sign of Félicité for the divine is likewise recognized. Hers is a personal image, the other, public. Elements of the real, tangible world are particularized to connote the supernatural in both cases.
It needs to be point out that, contrary to Reish's statement, the Eucharistic host in traditional Roman Catholic theology is much more than simply a "sign" of Christ.

13. Haig, "The Substance of Illusion," 315. One can scarcely imagine Haig citing Pécuchet's declaration as proof of the author's stance about the beliefs of such of his characters as Bournisien and Homais. In this same passage, Haig also maintains that "[Félicité's] world is ... thoroughly ambiguous in its final exaltation." Critical recourse to ambiguity, as Robert Francis Cook reminds us in *The Sense of the Song of Roland* (Ithaca and London: Cornell U. P., 1988, 180-181), can at times result from a discontinuity between the modern critic "at sea"—or, as I would suggest in the case under consideration, working in post-modern, secular oblivion—and the author's implied audience "at home" with the text, sharing certain knowledge and attitudes. In the case of *Un coeur simple*, Flaubert's readers, whether believers or not, were thoroughly imbued with a Catholic sensibility.

14. In Chapter 3 above, see the section on "The Sacraments" where I point out that in *Madame Bovary* it is only the Catholic rite of Extreme Unction which Flaubert presents in anything like a sympathetic light.

15. Fredric Jameson's observations about the readings of the endings of Flaubert's tales are helpful, although he goes too far in speaking of the "interminable generation of interpretive meanings" (80) in his article entitled "Flaubert's Libidinal Historicism," 76-83, in *Flaubert and Postmodernism*, ed. N. Schor and H. Majewski (Lincoln and London: University of Nebraska Press, 1984).

Conclusion

My colleague who asked me "What about the differences between *Madame Bovary* and *Thérèse Desqueyroux* [in addition to the similarities]?" might also have asked, but did not ask, another obvious question: "So what?" That too is an excellent question, and a fair one. An older school of literary criticism took very seriously the question of influence: Montaigne's influence on the *moralistes* of the following century; seventeenth- and twentieth-century playwrights' debts to classical sources in their plays which borrow and often reinterpret events from Greek and Roman history and myth; the Romantic discovery and appropriation of the Middle Ages. Even recent critical movements have continued to see value in source or influence studies, even while changing the terminology from "influence" to the more recondite "intertexuality."[1]

I started my study of these two novels because of the impression I had that Mauriac's novel of 1927 bore a remarkable resemblance to Flaubert's work published exactly seventy years earlier in 1857. The examination of the many similarities helps distill from these two seemingly distinctly different stories certain elements (themes, images, motifs) which enable each novelist to recount the life of an unhappily married woman whose existence seems bereft of much happiness at all or even of a sense of satisfaction at belonging to a family or social milieu and who, in the end, achieves none of the long sought-for feelings of *félicité*, *passion*, or *ivresse*, to use Flaubert's phrase. Whilst their social and economic stations are clearly different, their sexual orientations undeniably dissimilar, the ends of their stories quite divergent, Emma and Thérèse stand out in a long line of other such unhappily married women from Iseut to Phèdre to Anne Desbaresdes. These women are not, first and foremost, part of the vague and idealized "légion lyrique de ... femmes adultères" with whom Emma identifies after yielding to Rodolphe's sexual advances, but rather a cohort of remarkable, long-suffering spouses, unhappy with their lot in life and unable to extricate themselves from, what for them are, untenable situations. For both Emma and Thérèse, escape proves impossible, escape from family and social environment, but especially and more importantly, escape from their own unrealizable desires and their always more impracticable yearnings: Emma for yet another "félicité plus haute;" Thérèse for some accommodation with the irreconcilable, with "l'autre Thérèse."

I have tried, in this close textual study, to sketch out many of the similarities between Emma and Thérèse, yet there always seem to be more which, upon reflection, come to the fore. Readers will have their own lists. Consider, as examples, other similarities, not discussed in the preceding pages, but ones which some readers will surely have thought of. Emma and Rodolphe for the rendezvous (233) following their first love-making, as well as Thérèse and Azévédo for their first encounter (57), meet in a hut in the woods. Even when Emma and Thérèse hold diametrically opposite opinions, as they do on the type of fictional characters they prefer—Emma declares "Je déteste les héros communs et les sentiments tempérés, comme il y en a dans la nature (121); on the other hand, Thérèse "exécrait dans les romans la peinture d'êtres extraordinaires et tels qu'on n'en rencontre jamais dans la vie (54)—it is noteworthy that these two fictional characters both comment, in fact, on the sort of characters they themselves prefer in the novels they read. Then, there is the detail that both heroines smoke cigarettes. Smoking is for each of these woman a sign of social nonconformity. There are references throughout the novel to Thérèse's smoking. And the fact that she is deprived of her cigarettes during her retributive sequestration at Argelouse is surely not without significance. Emma uses cigarettes but twice. Each time she does, she does so in the company of one of her lovers. As Rodolphe begins to grow weary of her, she changes her usual behavior:

> Par l'effet seul de ses habitudes amoureuses, Mme Bovary changea d'allures. Ses regards devinrent plus hardis, ses discours plus libres; elle eut même l'inconvenance de se promener avec M. Rodolphe, une cigarette à la bouche, *comme pour narguer le monde*. (255)

Much later, in Rouen with Léon on the Thursday following the reinstatement of Emma's power of attorney, she is described this way:

> Quel débordement le jeudi d'après, à l'hôtel, dans leur chambre, avec Léon! Elle rit, pleura, chanta, fit monter des sorbets, voulut fumer des cigarettes, lui parut extravagante, mais adorable, superbe. (358)

While Tolstoy might be right that all happy families resemble one another, he is perhaps not totally correct when he contends that each unhappy family is unhappy in its own way. Surely Emma Bovary and Thérèse Desqueyroux share many of the same yearnings, the same feelings, the same unhappiness, and the same disappointments, and in ways and to degrees not explicable simply by the fact that each one is an unhappily married, provincial woman. These two remarkable women, fictional characters whose singular personalities make them seem more real to us than most of the people we actually know, occupy a unique place in the literary and emotional lives of their creators. For Flaubert, "Madame Bovary, c'est moi." Mauriac sees Thérèse on the sidewalk in Paris at novel's end and hopes she will be well. The story of neither woman's life ends well, however; yet, both Emma and Thérèse represent for readers exceptional human beings whose desires, aspirations, hopes, and yearnings speak to all of us about what it is to be human and thus engaged in a search—futile, perhaps, yet irrepressible—for *félicité*, *passion*, and *ivresse*.

NOTE

1. For a thorough review of the various meanings of intertextuality in structuralist and semiotic criticism, see Thaïs E. Morgan's "Is There an Intertext in this Text?: Literary and Interdisciplinary Approaches to Intertexuality," *American Journal of Semiotics* 3, no. 2 (1985): 1-40. Morgan evaluates the strengths and weaknesses and the ideological underpinnings of this concept in the thought of a number of contemporary critics (*inter alios*: Kristeva, Barthes, Riffaterre, Genette) and tries, if not to cut through, at least to label, the specimens in the "terminological jungle grown around intertextuality" (31). At least twice (23 and 31), Morgan notes how close Kristeva and Genette come to the source and influence studies associated with literary historicism.

Bibliography of Works Cited

Admussen, Richard, Edward J. Gallagher, and Lubbe Levin. "Novel into Film: An Experimental Course." *Literature/Film Quarterly* 6 (1978): 66-72.
Allen, Woody. "The Kugelmass Episode." *The New Yorker*, 2 May 1977, 34-39.
Augustin, Jean-Marie. *L'histoire véridique de la Séquestrée de Poitiers*. Paris: Fayard, 2001.
Balzac, Honoré de. *Le père Goriot*. Paris: Garnier-Flammarion, 1966.
Bart, Benjamin. *Flaubert*. Syracuse: Syracuse U. P., 1967.
Beizer, Janet. *Ventriloquized Bodies: Narratives of Hysteria in Nineteenth-Century France*. Ithaca and London, Cornell U. P., 1994.
Bloom, Harold. *The Anxiety of Influence: a Theory of Poetry*. New York: Oxford U. P., 1975.
Booker, John T. "*Indiana* and *Madame Bovary*: Intertextual Echoes." *Nineteenth-Century French Studies* 31, nos. 3 & 4 (2003): 226-236.
Bopp, Léon. *Commentaire sur Madame Bovary*. Neuchâtel and Paris: La Baconnière, 1951.
Bourgeois, André. "M. Homais, instrument du destin." *South Central Review* 28 (1968):124-126.
Brunswic, Anne; C. Bliet; and J.-P. Brighelli. *Flaubert: Madame Bovary*. Paris: Gallimard, 1993.
Bynum, Caroline Walker. *Jesus as Mother: Studies in the Spirituality of the High Middle Ages*. Berkeley: University of California Press, 1982.
Calinescu, Matei. *Rereading*. New Haven: Yale U. P., 1993.
The Catholic Encyclopedia. Edited by C. Harbermann, E. Pace, et al. 15 vols. New York: Appleton, 1907-1912.
Cook, Robert Francis. *The Sense of the Song of Roland*. Ithaca and London: Cornell U. P., 1988.
Crouzet, Michel. "Ecce Homais." *Revue d'Histoire Littéraire de la France* 89, no. 6 (1989): 980-1014.
Cuddon, J. A. *A Dictionary of Literary Terms*. Garden City, N. Y.: Doubleday, 1977.
Culler, Jonathan. *Flaubert: The Uses of Uncertainty*. Ithaca: Cornell U. P., 1974.
Curry, K. E. and L. R. Andrews. "Emma Bovary's Lost Brother: A Study of Flaubert's Use of 'Minor' Details in the Structure of *Madame Bovary*," *Nineteenth-Century French Studies* 25, nos. 1 & 2 (1996-1997): 92-99.
Danahy, Michael. *The Feminization of the Novel*. Gainesville: University of Florida Press, 1991.
Dane, Joseph. *Parody*. Norman and London: University of Oklahoma Press, 1988.

Diderot, Denis. *La religieuse*. Paris: Garnier-Flammarion, 1968.
Donaldson-Evans, Mary. "A Pox on Love: Diagnosing *Madame Bovary*'s Blind Beggar." *Symposium* 44, no. 1 (1990): 15-27.
Donnard, Jean-Hervé. *Trois Ecrivains Devant Dieu: Claudel, Mauriac, Bernanos*. Paris: Société d'Edition d'Enseignement Supérieur, 1966.
Fairlie, Alison. *Flaubert: Madame Bovary*. London: Edward Arnold, 1969.
Trevor Field. "The Split Personality of Eugène de Rastignac." *Romance Studies* 5 (1984): 167-81.
Flaubert, Gustave. *Correspondance*. Vol. III. Paris: Conard, 1926.
———. *Le Dictionnaire des idées reçues*. In *Oeuvres complètes*. Vol. II. Paris: Seuil, 1964.
———. "Dictionnaire des idées reçues." In *Oeuvres complètes*. Vol. VI. 528-584. Paris: Club de l'Honnête Homme, 1972.
———. *Madame Bovary*. Paris: Folio, 1972.
———. *Un coeur simple*. In *Trois contes*. Paris: Petits Classiques Larousse, 1965.
Genette, Gérard. *Figures III: discours du récit*. Paris: Seuil, 1972.
Gengembre, Gérard. *Gustave Flaubert: Madame Bovary*. Presses Universitaires de France, 1990.
Ginsberg, Michal P. *Flaubert Writing: A Study in Narrative Strategies*. Stanford: Stanford U. P., 1986.
Le Grand Robert de la Langue Française. 6 vols. Paris: Dictionnaires Le Robert, 2001.
Haig, Stirling. *Flaubert and the Gift of Speech: Dialogue and Discourse in Four Modern Novels*. Cambridge: Cambridge U. P., 1986.
———. "The Substance of Illusion in Flaubert's *Un coeur simple*." *Stanford French Review* 7, no. 3 (1983): 301-315.
Hale, Rosemary Drage. "Joseph as Mother: Adaptations and Appropriations in the Construction of Male Virtue." In *Medieval Mothering*, edited by J. C. Parsons and B. Wheeler, 101-116. New York: Garland, 1996.
Heath, Stephen. *Gustave Flaubert: Madame Bovary*. Cambridge: Cambridge U. P., 1992.
Hunt, Tony. "Fatality and the Novel: *Tristram, Manon Lescaut* and *Thérèse Desqueyroux*." *Durham University Journal*, n. s., 37, no 2 (1976): 183-195.
Jameson, Fredric. "Flaubert's Libidinal Historicism: *Trois Contes*." In *Flaubert and Postmodernism*, edited by Naomi Schor and Henry Majewski, 76-83. Lincoln and London: University of Nebraska Press, 1984.
Jenkins, Cecil. *Mauriac*. Edinburgh and London: Oliver and Boyd, 1965.
Joubert, André J. *François Mauriac et Thérèse Desqueyroux*. Paris: Nizet, 1982.
Kidd, William. "Oedipal and pre-Oedipal Elements in *Thérèse Desqueyroux*." In *François Mauriac: Visions and Reappraisals*, edited by John E. Flower and Bernard C. Swift, 25-46. Berg: Oxford, New York, Munich, 1989.

Kowieska, Elzbieta. "*Madame Bovary* et *Thérèse Desqueyroux*: L'Evasion Impossible." *Rocsniki Humanistyczne* 41, no. 5 (1993): 57-92.
LaCapra, Dominick. *Madame Bovary on Trial*. Ithaca and London: Cornell U. P., 1982.
Lacouture, Jean. *François Mauriac*. Paris: Seuil, 1980.
Lafayette, Madame de. *La Princesse de Clèves*. Paris: Garnier-Flammarion, 1996.
La Rochefoucauld, François de. *Maximes*. Edited by Jacques Truchet. Paris: Garnier, 1967.
Lloyd, Rosemary. *Madame Bovary*. London: Unwin Hyman, 1990.
Maraini, Dacia. *Searching for Emma: Flaubert and Madame Bovary*. Translated by Vincent J. Bertolini. Chicago and London: University of Chicago Press, 1998.
Mauriac, Claude. *Le Temps immobile*. Paris: B. Grasset, 1974.
Mauriac, François. *Bloc-notes III (1961-1964)*. Présentation et notes de Jean Touzot. Paris: Seuil, 1993.
———. *Oeuvres romanesques et théâtrales complètes*. Vol. II, edited by Jacques Petit. Paris: Gallimard, 1979. 4 vols, 1978-1985.
———. *Thérèse*. Translated by Gerard Hopkins. New York: Farrar, Straus and Giroux [Noonday paperback edition], 1972.
———. *Thérèse Desqueyroux*. Edited by Jean Collignon. Macmillan French Literature Series. New York: Macmillan, 1963.
Moloney, Michael F. *François Mauriac: A Critical Study*. Denver: Swallow, 1958.
Monaco, James. *How to Read a Film*. New York: Oxford U. P., 1977.
Monférier, Jacques. "Thérèse Desqueyroux, Phèdre et le destin." *RLM* 516-517 (1977): 109-118.
Morgan, Thaïs E. "Is There an Intertext in this Text?: Literary and Interdisciplinary Approaches to Intertexuality." *American Journal of Semiotics* 3, no. 2 (1985): 1-40.
The New Catholic Encyclopedia. 17 vols. New York: McGraw-Hill, 1967-1979.
Niess, Robert J. "On Listening to Homais." *French Review* 51 (1977): 22-28.
Orr, Mary. *Madame Bovary: Representations of the Masculine*. Bern: Peter Lang, 1999.
———. "Reflections on 'Bovarysme:' the Bovarys at Vaubyessard." *French Studies Bulletin* 61 (Winter 1996): 6-8.
Pasco, Allan H. *Allusion: a Literary Graft*. Toronto: University of Toronto Press, 1994.
Penrod, Lynn Kettler. "Focalization without (Too Much) Fuss: Using Narratology to Teach *Thérèse Desqueyroux*." *ADFL Bulletin* 19, no. 2 (1988): 7-12.
Perrault, Charles. *Contes de ma Mère Loye*. Edited by André Coeuroy. Paris: Editions de Cluny, 1948.

Phelan, James. "Why Narrators Can Be Focalizers—and Why It Matters." In *New Perspectives on Narrative Perspective*, edited by W. van Peer and Seymour Chatman, 51-64. Albany: SUNY Press, 2001.
Pierrard, Pierre. *Du Prêtre français au XIXe siècle, 1801-1905*. Paris: Hachette, 1986.
———. *Histoire des curés de campagne de 1789 à nos jours*. Paris: Plon, 1986.
Pochmann, Bernard. *Penance and the Anointing of the Sick*. New York: Herder and Herder, 1964.
Porter, Laurence M., ed. *A Gustave Flaubert Encyclopedia*. Westport, Ct.: Greenwood Press, 2001.
Porter, Laurence M. and Eugene F. Gray, ed. *Approaches to Teaching Flaubert's Madame Bovary*. New York: MLA, 1995.
Porter, Laurence M. and Eugene F. Gray, ed. *Gustave Flaubert's Madame Bovary: A Reference Guide*. Westport, Ct.: Greenwood Press, 2002.
Prévost, J.-L. *Le Prêtre, ce héros du roman*. Paris: Téqui, 1953.
Racine, Jean. *Phèdre*. Paris: Petits Classiques Bordas, 1970.
Raimond, Michel. *Le Roman contemporain: Le Signe du temps*. Paris: SEDES et CDU, 1976.
Raitt, Alan. "The Strange Case of Emma Bovary's Brother." *French Studies Bulletin* 66 (Spring 1998): 4-7.
Ramazani, V. K. *The Free Indirect Mode: Flaubert and the Poetics of Irony*. Charlottesville: University Press of Virginia, 1988.
Reid, James H. "Mauriac: the Ambivalent Author of Absence." *Studies in Twentieth-Century Literature* 2, no. 2 (1987): 167-188.
Reish, Joseph G. "'Those who see God' in Flaubert's *Trois contes*." *Renascence* 36, no. 4 (1986): 219-229.
Rhodes, James. "Homais, Capharnaüm, and *Madame Bovary*." *College English* 10, no. 1 (1983): 60-68.
Rubin, Miri. "Corpus Christi: Inventing a Feast." *History Today* 40 (July 1990): 15-21.
Sachs, Murray. "The Legacy of Flaubert." In *L'Hénaurme Siècle*, edited by Will L. McLendon. Heidelberg: C. Winter, 1984.
Schor, Naomi. *Breaking the Chain: Women, Theory, and French Realistic Fiction*. New York: Columbia U. P, 1985.
Schulz-Buschaus, Ulrich. "Homais oder die Norm des fortschrittlichen Berufsburgers: Zur Interpretation von Flauberts *Madame Bovary*." *Romanistisches Jahrbuch* 28 (1977): 126-149.
Segal, Naomi. *The Adulteress's Child: Authorship and Desire in the Nineteenth-Century Novel*. Cambridge, England: Polity Press, 1992.
Sherrington, R. J. *Three Novels by Flaubert*. Oxford: Oxford U. P, 1970.
Showalter, Elaine. *Sexual Anarchy: Gender and Culture at the Fin de Siècle*. New York: Viking, 1990.
Speaight, Robert. *François Mauriac: A Study of the Writer and the Man*. London: Chatto and Windus, 1976.

Speziale-Bagliacca, Roberto. *The King and the Adulteress: A Psychoanalytic and Literary Reinterpretation of Madame Bovary and King Lear.* Durham and London: Duke U. P., 1998.
Starkie, Enid. *Flaubert the Master.* New York: Atheneum, 1971.
Stoltzfus, Ben. "Point of view in *Un coeur simple*." *French Review* 35, no. 1 (1961): 19-25.
Sutton, Geneviève. "Phèdre et Thérèse Desqueyroux: une communauté du destin." *French Review* 43 (1970): 559-570.
Thibaudet, Albert. *Gustave Flaubert.* Paris: Gallimard, 1935.
Tooke, Adrianne. *Flaubert and the Pictorial Arts: From Image to Text.* Oxford: Oxford U. P., 2000.
Toulet, Suzanne. *Le Sentiment religieux de Flaubert d'après la correspondance.* Québec: Editions Cosmos, 1970.
Vargas Llosa, Mario. *The Perpetual Orgy: Flaubert and Madame Bovary.* Translated by H. Lane. New York: Farrar, Straus and Giroux, 1986.
Villon, François. *Complete Poems.* Translated by Barbara N. Sargent-Baur. Toronto, Buffalo, London: University of Toronto Press, 1994.
Williams, D. A. "Gender Stereotypes in *Madame Bovary*." *Forum for Modern Language Studies* 28, no. 2 (1992): 130-139.
———. *Psychological Determinism in Madame Bovary.* Occasional Papers in Modern Languages no. 9. Hull: University of Hull Publications, 1973.
———. "The Role of Binet in *Madame Bovary*." *Romanic Review* 71 (1980): 149-166.
Williams, Timothy. "Thérèse and Anne: Mauriac's Mimetic Rivals." *Romance Quarterly* 48, no. 2 (2001): 75-88.
Wuest, Joseph. *Matters Liturgical.* Translated by Thomas Mullaney. New York and Cincinnati: Frederick Pustet, 1956.
Zola, Emile. *L'Assommoir.* In *Les Rougon-Macquart.* Vol II. Paris: Bibliothèque de la Pléiade, 1961.

Index of Proper Names

I have not indexed the titles of the two novels I have studied; nor have I included the names of the major characters: Emma and Charles, Thérèse and Bernard; nor have I listed names which appear only once. Since the names of authors of books and articles are easily located in the Notes and in the Bibliography of Works Cited, these too have not been included in this Index.

Azévédo, Jean 18-20, 39, 40, 45n19, 77-79, 93, 95-97, 99n10, 103, 105, 106

Balzac, Honoré de 1, 7, 9, 78, 112, 113
Bellade, Julie 24, 98, 103, 106
Berthe 22, 26, 30-37, 44n11, 47, 59, 65, 69, 75, 112, 113
Binet 63, 76, 87
Blind man 4, 25, 52, 54, 58, 67, 73, 87, 119, 120
Bournisien 3, 4, 22, 31, 47-49, 52-69, 70n13, 71n15, 71n19, 71n20, 71n23, 73, 87, 122n13
Bouvard et Pécuchet 55, 119
Bovary (mère), Madame 30, 31, 57, 59, 60, 69, 75, 87, 112
Bovary (père), Monsieur 30, 47, 59, 60, 73, 87
Bovarysme (le) 4, 88, 109

Canaby, Madame (criminal) 14, 27n8, 38, 44n17
Clara, Tante 4, 16, 22, 25, 51, 77, 79, 86n14, 94, 98, 99n5
Colet Louise 71n19, 91, 106n1
Corpus Christi 48, 50, 51, 61, 116, 118, 119, 121n11

Curate (village priest in *Thérèse Desqueyroux*) 21, 45n19, 48, 50, 51, 69, 79, 95, 96-98

Delamare, Madame (criminal) 13, 14, 27n7
Dictionnaire des idées reçues (Le) 29, 30, 60, 62
Dubuc, la veuve 30, 112

Eucharist 47, 48, 50, 51, 56, 57, 116, 121n6
Eucharistic
  adoration 117
  Christ 118, 119
  experience 50
  fast 68
  host 50, 121n12
  parody 120
  procession 116
  transubstantiation 4, 118, 120
Extreme Unction 47, 48, 52-54, 56, 120, 122n14

Félicité (maid in *Madame Bovary*) 30, 68, 89
Félicité (main character in *Un coeur simple*) 4, 52, 61, 115-120, 121n10, 121n12, 122n13
Fête Dieu (La) see Corpus Christi

Index of Proper Names

Guillaumin 52, 75, 76

Hippolyte 18, 32, 36, 58, 62-64, 67, 98n1
Homais, Madame 3, 34, 88-92, 98
Homais, Monsieur 3, 16, 24, 37, 47, 48, 55-69, 70n14, 71n21, 73, 74, 87, 89, 90-92, 122n13

Immoraliste (L') 8, 96

Justin 69, 88-90, 92, 98, 98n1

Lagardy 19, 25, 64, 73, 87
La Rochefoucauld 7, 80
Larroque, Monsieur 79, 93-95
La Trave, Anne de 2, 18, 19, 38, 39, 41, 77,78, 93, 94, 97, 99n10, 104-106
La Trave (Les) 16, 24, 94, 97
La Trave, Madame de 14, 51, 78, 93, 95
La Trave, Monsieur de 77, 93, 94
Léon 2, 15, 17, 19, 20, 25, 29-31, 33. 34, 49, 56, 59, 60, 64, 69, 74-76, 89-91, 98n1, 101, 102, 109, 124
Lestiboudois 69, 90
Lheureux 29, 65, 75
Locuste (Sainte) 54, 95
Loulou 61, 115, 117-119, 121n12

Marie 22, 93, 103, 106, 107n5
Mass 4, 50, 51, 61, 68, 73, 74, 79, 118, 121n6

Père Goriot (Le) 1, 78, 112
Perruquier de Tostes (Le) 3, 87, 88, 92
Phèdre 7, 27n11, 38, 44n16, 123
Princesse de Clèves (La) 8, 101

Rodolphe 2, 15, 17-20, 23, 25, 29, 31-33, 44n13, 48, 49, 56, 57, 73, 75, 85n6, 90, 101, 102, 106, 109, 112, 123, 124
Rouault, Madame (referred to only as Emma's mother) 26, 31, 34, 36, 111, 112
Rouault, Monsieur 71n21, 74, 87, 111, 112

Séquestrée de Poitiers (La) 82, 85n11, 104, 106, 106n4

Un coeur simple 4, 52, 61, 115, 116, 119, 120, 120n2, 122n13

Zola, Emile 1, 7, 9, 27n11, 31